Beyond Expectation

David Reilly

Acknowledgments

I would like to thank a few people who helped me along the way with writing this book. Firstly, thanks to Ian Rankin for writing the foreword and for his support and encouragement over the years.   Thanks to Mark Tanner who edited the book for me and to Vicky Henderson who helped with the cover design.

For
Mum & Dad

Foreword

It will become clear to the reader of this book that David Reilly has tried never to let his Cerebral Palsy stand in the way of his ambition to both better himself and prove himself. He has endured everything from bullying at school through blinkered bureaucracy to struggles with his mental health and has done so with focussed determination. Along the way he becomes passionate about music and outdoor pursuits, and writes here with great depth of understanding about Scotland's wild landscape. When he's not cycling through it, he seems to be climbing it! His daily battles with discrimination are also recounted as he fights to be allowed to live his life on his own terms rather than those dictated by others. He reminds society that we should see beyond the disability to the potential. As the parent of a son with Special Educational Needs I was with David all the way as he set his sights on the grades that would allow him to attend a Further Education College, eventually gaining admission to the University of Manchester to study for a Molecular Biology MSc. Even when his mental health started to suffer, he refused to let life knock him down – reconnecting to nature helped him immeasurably and his love of the natural world shines through in the blog entries included here.

This short book is a testament of sorts, explaining the daily struggles of those with disabilities but also showing how courage and resilience can be found and fostered. David's is a story we can all learn from and enjoy.

Ian Rankin

Chapter 1

Early Days

If I were to ask my parents what I was like as a child they would say, "You were determined, stubborn and if you wanted to do something son, you would." From the very beginnings of my life, I have had a real determination to achieve what I wanted and not to be held back by my disability. At that time of course my achievements were the milestones that most children pass, sitting up, walking. and communicating. I haven't changed at all since those days. I am as determined as I ever was to do whatever I can to bring myself happiness. The difference is that what I do now are achievements that I, or more accurately my parents, would not have dared dream of being possible during those early years of my life.

By all accounts my entry into this world was extremely traumatic for everyone involved. All I can tell you about it for sure is that I was there. I believe mum nearly didn't make it and I was very, very ill. Most babies pop out and go straight into their mum's arms, but I went into an incubator and it was a whole forty eight hours before mum and I set eyes on each other. These precious moments at my birth had lifelong consequences. At around the age of nine months a paediatrician confirmed I had been starved of oxygen at birth and I was diagnosed as having Cerebral Palsy (CP).

And that was that!

My young parents had a really sick baby on their hands and more or less just had to get on with it.

It really was the start of a journey into the unknown. Medics had no idea as to the extent of my brain damage. Whether I would walk, talk, or have any sort of learning disability was anyone's guess. It would be a very long road whatever it would be. My parents were given very little if any support in those days. It was the early 1970's and disability was not known about as well as it is now. I saw paediatricians from time to time who measured or monitored my progress. Community physiotherapists and occupational therapists would come round to the house and carry out exercises with me. My parents would do this every day to try to strengthen and tone my muscles. As well as the therapists I had various bits of equipment to try and help me learn to walk. Thanks to my parents' methodical daily exercises with me, I grew stronger and stronger. There are not many photographs of me as a baby, but there are some. A later photograph shows me hanging on to a walking frame when I must have been about two. I remember mum talking about a frame they had when I was really young and I used to dangle my feet on the ground.

Of course, my parents have told me lots of stories about myself when I was small. One of the stories that I love and sticks out in my mind was that of my Christening or Baptism. My parents were churchgoers in those days. My dad was a Boy's Brigade Captain and my mum played the organ on a Sunday. Church, and presumably Faith, was a significant part of their lives. Their minister was around at the time of my birth. So the story goes that when it came to my Christening, knowing the right side of my body was damaged, the minister put the Blessed Water on the left side of my precious head. This little story makes the hairs on the back of my neck stand on end. Faith became a part of my life and created the person I am. Spirituality is now so important to my life.

One day, at the age of four, I took my first steps. Most children walk at about two years old but for me it took longer to find my feet. Even then, they said that I would trip over a matchstick. My balance was not good at that time and I wore a helmet around the house to protect my head when I fell over. I don't know how long it took me to find it, but balance is still not my forte. It was however the very beginning of a long journey that would be taken moment by moment, one day at a time. To achieve anything was a methodical step by step process not unlike my life today. It took planning, practice, repetition and discipline. Lessons learned right there in infancy would stick with me for a lifetime.

My first Bicycle

I cannot remember the age I would have been when I first learned to ride a bike but it took me a long time to learn to ride on two wheels. I think my first bike had stabilisers and then after that I seem to remember having a trike. We lived in a nice housing estate which had next to no traffic and lots of wide footpaths that were ideal for children to ride on. There was a large hill down into the estate and we would cycle up that and ride back down. It was a safe environment where I must have just loved being on my bike. As I grew bigger, I became more and more determined to be like everyone else and ride a two wheeled bike. Two stabilisers became one and then I was able to ride two wheeled. It was such an achievement and astonishing to many. It remains a surprise to many even today that I can sometimes struggle to move around and get up off my feet but give me two wheels and I can ride all day. I don't know if I even understand it myself but riding a bike is one of my greatest joys. I began to ride on two wheels and over time bikes just became a bigger and bigger part of my life. I would cycle to and from school and all around Haddington to see friends or just for a run. If I wasn't riding my bike I would be taking it to bits, cleaning it and putting it back together. I just loved my bike and everything about it. Bikes have always been a vital, beneficial part of my life.

First taste of the Outdoors

I grew up in the small market town of Haddington in East Lothian. Haddington in those days was a sleepy quiet country town half the size it is today. It was a wonderful place to grow up and it still holds an enormous amount of affection in my heart. East Lothian is a beautiful county with rolling hills on one side and long stretches of sandy beaches on the other. It provided a wonderful place for children to experience their first taste of the outdoors and the seaside. And that's exactly what happened. My mum and dad were really interested in the outdoors and exploring the countryside. From as early as I can remember, weekends were spent walking through beautiful hills and forests, or combing the wonderful beaches of the East Lothian coastline. Of course I wasn't doing the walking there but rather being carried. As I type this, I can see in mind's eye the old grey and navy canvas contraption they would put me in and load me onto dad's back. It was fine until I grew bigger and heavier. I think eventually Dad fell onto some rocks while transporting me on his back. I wasn't hurt but dad twisted his ankle so he really couldn't carry me much after that. We were then given, presumably by physiotherapy, something we called 'The Buggy.' It was just like a large pushchair for an older child and oh how I used to resent having to go in it. But, it meant we could get out and about and continue to enjoy the outdoors as much as we could.

The town of Haddington where I grew up had a large Scouting movement in those days and, to the best of my knowledge, it still has. I started off in Cubs at an early age, went through to Scouts and then onto Venture Scouts. Haddington was really lucky to have

12

many boys involved and many willing volunteers to run it. East Lothian was like a playground with a multitude of places to go hillwalking or kayaking right on our doorstep. We really had some wonderful times and lots of fun camping or travelling to places in the back of the Scout van affectionately named 'Tin Ribs.' I felt included in the Scouts but at the same time my frustration would come to the surface if I wasn't allowed to do something or take part. The irony is that the things I became frustrated about, not being permitted or able to do then, are the very things that I spend my life doing now.

For example each winter the Scouts would make a ski trip to Glenshee for the day. The very idea of me going with them or trying to ski was considered ridiculous and absolutely out of the question. Nobody could have thought that thirty years later I would go to Glenshee, put skis on and develop a real passion for skiing. This would be followed up with many trips to the Alps. It was a different era though and in the early 1980's disability sport didn't exist the way it does now. The notion of someone with CP going to learn to ski would have been just ridiculous. Of course I was not as fit and able then as I am now.

At that time in my life, I remember the Scouting movement being a real kind of an oasis for me because other areas of my life were not as easy. Although it was a safe place, there were still aspects creeping in that reflected what was going on elsewhere. There was another boy in Scouts who without doubt had a learning disability. I used to resent being grouped together with him.

If the others were doing something difficult or challenging, we would have to entertain each other with different activities. I used to resent that, but I know now it was nothing compared to the prejudice I would go on to face in the future. I was beginning to become aware of people's attitudes and perceptions as it was. People's instant judgments usually concluded that I had a learning disability and they would treat me, or talk to me accordingly in a patronising or ignorant way. As a point of interest, I hope you are noticing the language I am using here. There was no learning disability! You were labelled mentally handicapped or physically handicapped! Language is so important and these words seriously grate on me now just as much as they did back then. That was the accepted norm and I spent so much of my childhood trying to show I had a physical disability rather than a learning disability. This is the hideous fact that would follow me for most of my life

Early School Days

I started primary one at Haddington Infant School in 1976 at the age of five. I can still hear in my head the hymns we would sing in assembly in the early days of P1. I never seemed to like the school environment from the start. and it gradually grew more and more challenging for me. Unable to communicate well in those days, school attendance seemed to be interspersed with trips to the local Educational Psychology department. I don't think anybody knew, in those days, what I was capable of. Whether or not I was able to learn at the same rate as my peers was an unknown. But it didn't take long before my parents had confirmation that I was of above average intelligence and that I deserved the same chance of learning as everyone else. It was my physical limitations that let me down or indeed began to cause me phenomenal frustration.

Being in primary three is the first memory I have of difficulties in the classroom. Despite seeing an occupational therapist, I was struggling to write. Even holding a pencil was difficult and it was beginning to hold me back. In the days of doing sums longhand, the teacher began to write my sums out for me and hand them to me to complete, which I did in good time. Writing was beginning to pose serious issues for me, and it became a source of frustration when other children would complete tasks far faster than me. Another real point of crisis that was beginning to creep in was the school playground. Children are very cruel to each other and the name calling, taunting and ridicule began, and it would continue for many years.

My parents and anybody who knew me really, would try to think of ways to help me develop either physically or in the classroom, or in any way they could. I was still very unstable on my feet in those days, balance being a real problem. It might even have been before I was at school, someone had an idea that swinging a golf club might help me learn and improve my balance. So a relative or someone close to the family went to the trouble of acquiring an old club, cutting it to my size and putting a grip on. I was still tiny at the time. This turned out to be the start of a lifelong love affair between me and the game of Golf. I spent the whole of my childhood and my teenage years playing Golf, I was daft about it as they say. We'll see later how golf has always been part of my life.

Thinking about it, this is such a great lesson in doing something just because you love it. I started swinging a golf club to help my balance, but over time it became a part of who I was. Many people do things because they think it might open doors, lead to opportunities, or ultimately make money. The best reason for doing anything is because it makes you happy. If you are happy doing what you are doing, then it is more likely to open doors or create opportunities. I have come across people who have what I consider great businesses, a lifestyle business that they created to lead the life they want to lead. If you ask how they got started, most will say it was a hobby, or it grew out of a hobby. Ask why it was their hobby and they'll say because they loved doing it, it is as simple as that. When we do something we truly love then that comes across to others. When our hearts are not in it, it becomes like the same salesman who is trying to sell a product he doesn't really believe in. You can spot it a mile away. As soon as you find and follow your passion, doors open for you.

Another instance where doing something to help just became a part of life was in the field of music. I was in primary two, about seven years old. Once a week in the afternoon, my mum would pick me up early from school and take me to Music Therapy. We would go to a small village outside Haddington called Bolton where I would spend an hour or so with Mrs Cartwright. At that time Music Therapy was something new and not well known about at all. I am still not sure why music therapy was recommended to my parents, but it was, and I am so grateful for that now. It turns out that my teacher, Mrs Cartwright, was an absolute pioneer of Music Therapy in the UK and she was responsible for introducing it to Scotland. I wish I had understood then, what a privilege it was to be taught by her. I can clearly remember the old, converted byre that was her home. She would let me clang cymbals, bang drums and make any noise that took my fancy. It was a wonderful and valuable experience and it started my passion for music. I have always had difficulty with fine motor movements so although music has been a joy, it has also been a source of considerable frustration. I have tried dozens of different types of instruments over the years, guitar, piano and violin to name but a few. I can just about create a tune out of most of them but I am a master of none.

I have always loved listening to and playing music. My frustration over music was probably at its greatest levels during my teens when I really wanted to be able to play. I took piano lessons for a while but with only the use of one finger on the right hand, and very little control of it at that, I suspect frustration got the better of me. But I am very grateful for the time I spent learning whatever I could.

Today my approach to music is very different and I experience sheer joy from it. I still play lots of instruments but I play them for sounds, not tunes. Sound heals our innermost being and making sound of any sort for me is therapy. I don't need to try to play tunes perfectly or to follow sheet music of any sort. I find this a nice analogy for life now. I do not need to follow other people's rules to try to meet anyone else's expectations. I do not need to dance to their tune, or indeed any tune at all. It is so liberating to open the floodgates and to drink deeply from the wells of our own creativity. Then we can become fully connected with ourselves and be the people we are meant to be. Creativity is one of our greatest gifts. Music has really helped shape my life. Some music I have heard recently for the first time, other bands I have been listening to since childhood. I have to thank my parents for exposing me to a wide range of music when I was really small. Hearing this now sometimes recreates memories for me of the home I grew up in.

Mum and Dad had seen a very young Nigel Kennedy at the Usher Hall in Edinburgh. Long before he became well known, my folks saw him play Tchaikovsky's Violin Concerto. Every time I hear that, it puts me right back there. I am so grateful that they opened my mind to classical music at such a young age because it has stuck with me all my life. Another musician I have respected and listened to all of my life is Paul Simon. One of my earliest memories of music is listening to Simon and Garfunkel's 'Mrs Robinson ' in my parent's front room. From that time on I have always loved Paul Simon and he has remained with me all the way through my adult life.

As well as having Music therapy, I did other activities outside of school time to try and help my balance or general development. I can just remember going to Riding for the Disabled in those days on a farm outside of Haddington.

I guess by this time age differences between my physical abilities and that of other children were becoming pronounced. School playgrounds, PE classes and Sports days weren't much fun for me and the name calling and bullying could seem relentless at times. During these early years, I was constantly being monitored by Paediatricians in Edinburgh. Every so often I would be off school and have to travel into Edinburgh to the Sick Kids Hospital or even worse the then called Scottish Spastics Society. Oh, how I used to resent being taken to the Spastic Society, but that is what it was called in these days and when I was a kid, it did not feel right. It just shows you how important language is and how acceptable and unacceptable labelling changes over time. Spastic was a genuine medical term for someone with Cerebral Palsy. It only became a nasty word because it been used so much in a derogatory fashion. I am glad to see the word is not used any more. It was very distasteful then and it is very distasteful now. But, you may not believe this, once I was in a ski resort on my own. I stopped for a coffee and I asked someone to carry my drink to a table for me. I can hardly walk in my ski boots, let alone carry a drink! I sat down next to them and they were a really lovely family from the Netherlands. We had a nice chat over coffee and later in the proceedings she said, 'Are you spastic?' and I said 'yes.' It was the most bizarre thing!. She would not have meant it the way we think of it. Again, it just tells us a lot about language and what is acceptable for some, might be extremely offensive to others.

I was at the end of infant school and about to go into primary 4. But P4 was in a different place, with different teachers and a different headmaster. The head was nearing retirement and had quite narrow, fixed views regarding disability. At the school where I was about to start Primary 4 there was a special unit for children with learning disabilities. The head at the time wrote to my parents to inform them that I would be joining that class on arrival at the school. There was no debate or an invitation to meet me first before that was to take place.

Thankfully, my parents did not let it happen! They fought for me to stay in the class I had been in and eventually it was agreed that I could stay in a mainstream class. This would turn out to be the first of a series of battles my parents would have to take up just to allow me a fair chance at an education. However, things were about to become more challenging for me and over the next few years wider gaps would appear between myself and the other able-bodied children.

Despite the challenges, difficulties, and barriers I was experiencing, and was going to experience with education, we still maintained a fantastic family life. We did all sorts of outdoor activities at the weekend and a lot of our lives were spent outdoors. Mum and dad took us camping when we were quite young. I remember the family tent and the trusty trailer that dad used to put everything in and tow behind our car. We toured large parts of Scotland and had some wonderful times. One year however we were washed out in a storm and we had to give up the tent for a static caravan. The caravan was right on the seafront and not so far from where we lived. We spent many fabulous freedom weekends and holidays there and it was pure joy. We spent long days out on the beach, perusing intriguing rock pools or in the river looking for fish. Fishing became a really important hobby for us all. We started off fishing from the harbour wall or from a beach but eventually my dad acquired a small boat and we would venture out to sea in it. We came back with an abundance of fish in those days. Family life was really good and we had so much fun. I was lucky enough to have a really supportive and protective bigger brother. He was full of care, kindness and understanding towards me. Sometimes, if other children were bullying me, as they did, he would really put himself on the line to stand up for me. I am forever in his debt for this.

As we grew older we continued to have a really active family life and great holidays together. After many wonderful times at the caravan, we went on our first holiday abroad. The four of us went to the Greek island of Crete for a week which was so exciting at the time. First time on a plane and experiencing a different country, food and culture. We had a fantastic time. This turned out to be the first of a few foreign holidays we had as a family, the pinnacle being the final one we had all together when we travelled to Australia in 1989. My dad's brother and family lived in Brisbane and we went to spend a month with them. Stopping in Singapore on the way, we spent time soaking up the culture, heat and humidity. I can still remember leaving the plane and the heat just engulfing you as soon as you step out. It felt amazing. Singapore was, as still is so far, the most different culture I have experienced. The sounds and smells have given me a real desire to travel again. It was so nice to spend time with family in Australia then. The highlight was a week we hired a yacht and sailed around the Whitsunday Islands. Real special family times that are so memorable.

Having such a supportive family turned out to be invaluable in the troubles and difficulties that were to follow. Nobody could even have predicted or foreseen what lay ahead. Most of us in the western world accept Education as a Right. A chance to learn, to develop intellectually, to eventually sit exams, is taken as a given for most of us. For me, however, this wasn't so. I had been boxed up and labelled as a child with learning difficulties. My parents would have to fight tooth and nail just to allow me the same chances and opportunities to learn as every other child.

Chapter 2

King's Meadow school took children from the beginning of primary 4 until the end of P7 after which, children would go on to the local secondary school, Knox Academy. It was soon time for me to go on to King's Meadow and arrangements were being made. The headmaster at the time was adamant that I should be in the special class. There was already a special class in the school for disabled children and many of them had a learning disability. My parents had to fight really hard to keep me in a mainstream classroom.

I began primary four in a mainstream class and things were about as good as they could be. As time wore on I started struggling more and more with my school work and the playground continued to be a battlefield. The name calling and bullying persisted and I just couldn't bear to be at school and I started to run away. My mum would drop me off and I would go in through the front door of the school, straight down the corridor and straight out again at the back door. I would wander around Haddington until my mum got a phone call from one of her many looksouts. After this she would come and find me and take me back to school. It felt like this went on for years. I hated school and being there was just torture. I would lock myself in the bathroom, pretending to be ill, just to get out of going to school.

After struggling as long as I could tolerate in mainstream education, it was decided that I should go to a special school in Edinburgh. I remember the day I first went to visit the school. It must have been in the depths of winter because the snow was falling heavily. Everyone seemed happy, pleased to see me and welcoming. It was like a breath of fresh air from the torment that I endured in my mainstream Haddington school. After a short discussion it was decided I would start school at Graysmill, and I did in the January 1983. I think I would have been around 11 or 12 years old when, for the first time in years, I was enjoying school and I was happy again. The next few years would go a long way towards defining the rest of my life, in the same way any child is shaped during these precious teenage years.

The truth is that I reckon I could write an entire book about my time at Graysmill school, or at least fill up many pages of this book with the story. I am not going to do that and I am going to keep it as short as I possibly can. I do not think it would add much to the mood of this book and it certainly will not do me much good to try and regurgitate it all. So instead, I'll just say what I think needs to be said to support this part of my story.

The longer I spent at Graysmill school the more my behaviour started to deteriorate. I was struggling with school work and becoming more and more frustrated. Other members of the class seemed to be able to read, write and understand things far easier than I could. I used to become extremely frustrated and find myself in trouble. I would run away, or again lock myself in the bathroom in the morning hoping that I wouldn't have to go to school. I would lash out at people and eventually I was expelled or excluded from school. After a while I was reinstated but this time into a class of children with learning disabilities.

My parents were not happy about this. They could not understand why I had been put into a class for children with learning disabilities. They did not think I was a genius or anything but they certainly knew I did not have a learning disability. There had to be another problem somewhere. My parents knew it was with the school and the learning environment and of course the school thought I had learning disabilities and all the problems were at home. The battles raged on for years, and I spent the best part of two years not going to school at all! By this time, I had made endless trips to see Educational Psychologists and Child Psychiatry who more or less backed up my parents. I didn't have a learning disability, I was not stupid, and if anything was I was above average intelligence.

Everything eventually made sense however when, after assessment with a child psychologist, they diagnosed me as having Dyslexia !

No wonder I wasn't able to read or write!

I had never been taught with the specialist help I needed. And, I would never receive the help I needed from Graysmill school. Instead they maintained I had learning disabilities and they were not about to give me the opportunity to prove otherwise. Further tough battles continued to rage on between my parents and the Education Department. As I understand, it was all about my 'Record of Educational Need.' Every disabled child had a Record of Needs and mine read that I had 'Significant Learning Difficulty' meaning I had learning disability or was mentally disabled or handicapped (as they used that ghastly word in these days). My Record of Need should have stated that I had 'Significant *specific* learning difficulty' which meant something quite different. Specific learning difficulty meant dyslexia, or dysgraphia.

My parents went all the way with the supreme challenge of applying to the Secretary of State for Scotland to arrange for my Record of Need to be formally altered. They were the first people in Scotland ever to do so.

I left school the moment I could, days after my 16th birthday with not a single qualification to my name but with an invitation to a local day centre where I could sew mailbags and make Christmas cards for the rest of my days.

My adult life had been effectively written off before it had even been given a chance.

Throughout all of this I did of course have things that I liked, hobbies and things that kept me sane. The golf club that someone gave me as a small child in order to try and help me balance had developed into a love of golf. I spent most of my early teenage years playing and thinking about golf. East Lothian is a wonderful place to play and its coast is home to some of the finest courses in the world. Haddington has a lovely golf course and I remember receiving my first junior season ticket at around the age of 12 or 13. My mum and dad spent half their life giving me lifts up and down to the golf course. As I grew stronger and fitter, I kept my clubs in a locker there and I used to cycle to and from the course. I remember the long summer evenings playing until it was almost dark and I could hardly see the ball. Golf was a really big thing for me. I remember being taken to see the British Open just a few miles away when it was played at Muirfield.

Music was becoming more important for me too although my relationship with music was becoming more difficult as time went on. Being so musical I was really keen to play an instrument and I had tried lots of different instruments. The difficulty was that with any sort of instrument it required control of fine motor movement and I just didn't have the dexterity in my fingers for it. I remember going to piano lessons for a while and I had a really lovely teacher. I only had control, and even then not much control, of one finger on my right hand. Despite the tutor doing her best to find pieces that would suit predominantly the left hand, frustration crept in and often got the better of me. I remember years later asking my mum why she got rid of the piano and she said it was because it was making me so unhappy. Presumably the frustration of trying to play things and not being able to was just too much. I wish I had felt better about it then as I do now, or perhaps that would have been putting an old head on young shoulders. Now, I just don't care whether or not I can play tunes, I just like making noise with any instrument. I am not sure whether or not the noises sound nice to other people, but they are my sounds and they make me happy. I receive my music therapy this way.

Listening to music was however a different experience. As a teenager I was enjoying listening to rock music and buying more and more records. I was really into heavy rock, and I still am, and I am so grateful that I held onto my records all this time. As CD's became more popular in the late 1980's, many people parted with their records but not me! I loved buying rock records and asking for them for my birthday and Christmas. One year, I must have been about 12 or 13, my grandmother asked me what I would like for Christmas. I replied, in my squeaky unbroken voice, that I wanted *'The Great Rock n' Roll Swindle, by the Sex Pistols.'* To her credit she walked into the record store on Princes Street and bought it for me. It did go some way to making up for the 'Shaking Stevens' record she gave me the year before!

I have always had an eclectic taste. I remember my brother taking me to my first rock concert, 'AC/DC' at the Edinburgh Playhouse. I must have had an interest in Jazz in those days as well because my mum took me to concerts at the Edinburgh Jazz festival. Music has always been a really big thing for me and I am so thankful I was introduced to such a wide variety at such an early age.

Interestingly, another thing I remember being involved in at that time was a small Christian group in a local church. I cannot remember how it came about that I was going along there. Although my parents had been great church goers in their youth, my brother and I were not regularly taken to church and it was not something we did very often. I remember going to Sunday School sometimes, or if we had been marching with the Scout Troupe or Armistice Day for example. But there must have been something that connected with me to make me go on a regular basis to prayer group. Of course, as a result many of my friends were Christians and I spent my time hanging out with them. For someone who was not actively brought up in the church, I was developing my Faith and thinking about what it all meant.

A New Beginning

Thankfully, in November 1987 I was given another chance and the glimmer of a much-needed opportunity. My parents had been made aware of a specialist further education college in Coventry in the Midlands. It was a long way from home but my options were limited at that time. I was still more or less unable to read or write then at the age of 16 and was clearly never going to obtain the help I needed anywhere in Scotland. I travelled south to visit the college and attend an interview. It was a breath of fresh air. I stayed there for the night and met teaching staff, care staff and other students. It was a different environment altogether. I would be away from home, living in student accommodation and having lessons on site. It all looked fantastic except I needed special remedial teaching that the college did not have the resources to provide. Despite it being a positive experience, the college didn't think they were the right place for me.   We drove home to Scotland feeling downhearted and disappointed because options up here were next to none. My prospects were looking very bleak indeed.

A few days later my parents took a telephone call from the vice-principal of Hereward College. They had found someone in Coventry with the necessary skills to give me the remedial teaching that I required. They were prepared to admit me to the college and bring in the remedial teaching that I needed. That was that, an offer I couldn't refuse. I cannot remember the time scale but I think it was in a matter of a couple of weeks I was down in Coventry in late November 1987. I can still remember very clearly standing in the car park waving my parents off with one hand and my guitar tucked under the other. It was the start of a whole new chapter in my life.

Chapter 3

Settling into college life at the age of 16 was difficult. I was a long way from home with strangers and of course I was homesick and unhappy for a while. I do remember being on the telephone to my parents asking them to come and get me and take me home. It took me a long time to settle but I slowly got there and started to enjoy college life. Students stayed in dormitories in either twin or single rooms and there was a student union that provided regular social events. There were students there from all over the UK, and indeed the world, and I started to make some really good friends with other students and staff. Some of the staff, particularly the care staff, were there for all the right reasons and had all our well-being at heart. Others were not, and that was something you just had to learn, accept and put up with. It was an amazing experience and I was lucky to be there because, most of all, I got the chance of an Education that I was denied in Scotland.

I cannot remember how I chose the subjects I wanted to study. Hereward College had a fairly broad range of subjects to choose from and students were studying all sort of things. It was taken for granted that I would do Maths and English and the rest was up to me. I chose the sciences. I started with Biology and Chemistry, then eventually Physics as well. I had enjoyed Science at Graysmill school so it seemed like the right thing to do to study science.

As well as my classes, and arguably more importantly, I started remedial class. I had a lovely tutor called Olivia who I would spend five hours with every week. I can still remember how we started right at the very beginnings of the English language. I was 16 years old and learning sounds like a child in early primary school might do. I was reciting basic sounds like 'Th th th and Ch ch ch.' I was 16 but I had to start from scratch. I could not believe I was doing this at my age. This seemed to go on for months, or at least it felt like it did. But what started as 5 hours remedial teaching per week eventually became 3 hours and I was beginning to make great progress.

I was working hard at my studies and really enjoying the sciences and in particular Biology. I had a fantastic tutor who brought the subject alive and really encouraged my enthusiasm for Biology. So much so, that it was decided that I would sit my GCSE Biology in the first year. It was the opportunity that I, or my parents, thought would never come, the chance to sit a public exam. I still have a copy of the letter the headmaster of Graysmill School wrote to my parents stating that I has learning disabilities and would never sit a public exam. Eight months after starting at Hereward College I sat my GCSE Biology and I achieved grade B. Could this be the turnaround people wondered, could this be the opportunity I needed to prove everyone wrong? That is what it felt like I had to do at this time, to prove to people I did not have learning difficulties.

I was doing well at my studies but in communities like the small town of Haddington, people had already made up their minds. For as long as I can remember people have generally treated me as learning disabled. It was very subtle but it was my reality and it would happen all the time. People would speak more slowly to me, use hand signs, or speak more loudly to me, as if I did not understand. It has happened all my life, and it still happens most days in shops, restaurants and public places. If anyone appears to have any sort of physical impairment, particularly around communication, people tend to assume learning disabled. In the small town where I grew up this attitude was everywhere. Although I was made welcome and included in local activities such as the Scouts, the majority I suspect thought I was learning disabled and treated me accordingly. It used to frustrate and torment me terribly and has been possibly the one thing I would change if I had the chance. I have always said if I could, I would change my verbal communication. Although I am perfectly audible and people can understand me mostly now, it has not always been the case. I suspect my speech was even more laboured when I was a child. I have always found it difficult at times to extract my words. The physical struggle it was at times to form my words and project them used to be tortuous. It was always made worse by people's impatience and the speed at which they would complete my sentences for me. Although I find communication much easier now, I still avoid certain situations such as crowded places or where there can be background noise.

We make judgments about others all the time, I do it myself. If people are different in any way, or indeed impaired in some way, we make instant judgements about them. We are human beings. How many times have you heard it said that an employer makes his decision during the first thirty seconds of an interview, first impressions are everything. That then, I suspect, has been to my detriment because I have generally always been judged or labelled as being learning disabled. If we were to talk about chips on shoulders or hang ups this one would be my major, painful issue. But, as the saying goes, like every well-balanced Scotsman, I have a chip on both my shoulders. I felt like I had so much to prove from as far back as I can remember and this has stuck with me all of my life.

Throughout my time at Hereward College, I remained really focused on acquiring an education. I don't really know where it came from and it certainly didn't feel like pressure. I had a deep-rooted desire to be educated, and prove the world wrong. After completing my GCSE Biology, I spent the next years preparing for the rest of my GCSEs in Maths and English and the other Sciences. GCSE English of course was always going to be difficult for me. My remedial work continued but reading and writing comprehension was challenging. Thankfully at the time my tutor found a GCSE syllabus that was completed by coursework only, there was no final exam and no time pressure. This was the best course for me given that I was still miles behind with my English comprehension. I still wasn't reading much in those days but I do remember having to study books and read stories as a class. I can remember the very first time I actually enjoyed and appreciated the contents of a book. It was ' The Odour of Chrysanthemums ' by

D.H. Lawrence. I can still remember reading it in class and actually enjoying it. Up until then books had been my enemy, given me restless nights and endless frustration. I used to throw books across my bedroom floor because I wanted to read them, wanted to understand them, but could not.

I was preparing for four GCSE exams that year and working as hard as I could. Things were great academically but I was struggling with the social side of college life, I was never good at that.

Despite not being happy and wanting to pack up and go back to Scotland I was so focused on extending my education it was a means to an end. That year I attained GCSEs in the other four subjects and it was time to choose my A level subjects. Having sat GCSE Biology the year before I was already studying A level Biology and loving it. It was my favourite subject and I had a fantastic tutor. It seemed obvious then for me to go on and study for A level Chemistry and Physics and so that is what I did. I had another excellent, talented tutor who taught me both Chemistry and Physics and she really inspired me in the sciences.

Before I knew it, I was seriously thinking about applying to University. I had already sat A level Biology and passed, and I just had to complete Chemistry and Physics and that was me in. Choosing a subject was not difficult. I loved Biology and had done from day one and so I chose this to continue studying. At that time, Biotechnology was relatively new and one of the most exciting areas of modern science. This was 1990 and the genome was just beginning to be unlocked and discovered. The implications of this would turn out to be huge. I applied and had interviews at a number of different Universities including UCL being my first choice.

I didn't make it into UCL but at the end of four years, and a lot of hard work at Hereward College I had completed the entry requirements for University. It was an amazing feeling!

To have had my adult life written off totally and to categorise me as a slow learner, someone who would never sit an exam, it was quite an amazing turn around. People, and more importantly the education department in Scotland, had got it seriously wrong and I did not have learning disabilities.

I was Dyslexic and I required specialist teaching in order to overcome it.

I left Hereward College in 1991 after securing a place at

The University of Abertay on a four-year degree course in Biotechnology.

It was the breakthrough I had always wanted. It was my passion.

It is difficult to overestimate the effects my difficult education had on all of my family. Unfortunately, during these challenges, my older brother was going through crucial years in his education. My parents were so focused on my problems, battling and trying to procure the best possible teaching for me that they inevitably spent most of their time trying to resolve my issues. As a result, my brother probably lost out in terms of their attention at crucial times. Fortunately, and to his credit, he has gone on to be phenomenally successful in his chosen field of business.

After discovering that my difficulties had been due to undiagnosed Dyslexia, my mum became involved with local Dyslexia support groups. Before long she was supporting other parents with dyslexic children and the home phone was becoming a telephone helpline. My mum would spend hours on the phone listening to parents who had children who were struggling at school. Parents could be distraught and at their wits end not knowing what to do or how to obtain help for their child.

Many of their children were hating school and trying their hardest to avoid school, or running away as I had done in the past. The same patterns of behaviour were cropping up as children continued to struggle to get the help they needed. Dyslexia and in particular the counselling aspect took a bigger role in my mum's life. After having been involved in a local Dyslexia group in East Lothian, news started to spread. She was giving talks to doctors and teachers about Dyslexia and the effects on the family. She was asked to speak at conferences both locally and internationally. She eventually took the chair of the Scottish Dyslexia Association which later became 'Dyslexia in Scotland'. At the same time as she was working with Dyslexia, and in order to be able to support other parents, mum studied to become a fully qualified counsellor. Starting with the very basic studies mum worked very hard and attained a postgraduate qualification in counselling. My mother worked tirelessly between her dyslexia work and counselling studies for over twenty years and I feel that she truly does deserve a medal for all her fantastic efforts.

Chapter 4

Isn't it funny how music can remind you of happenings and puts you in places from the past. It can be a particular track or an album that takes your mind away to another place. Without thinking I can put on a CD and be transported right back to my room in my first year at university.

It is a nice feeling. Those were very happy days and some of the best times of my life. I had a lot of fun and met a lot of great people, some of whom I'm still in contact with today. When I first went to Dundee, I moved into a hall of residence called Mayfield Hall, where I would spend the first two years of my course. Mayfield no longer exists sadly and now a housing estate stands on the site where it once was. It was a pretty big hall that was home to a couple of hundred students and it was set in really nice grounds. One of my bedrooms had a lovely view over the front lawn across the river Tay. I can see it all now on a beautiful cold and crispy frosty morning.

I can still remember the very first night I arrived in the halls of residence. The university had laid on two double decker buses that we all piled into and were taken down to the Marketgate, the home of the student union. It was the first of countless nights of fun, drinking, dancing and socialising. Halls of residence were a great place to get to know people and make new friends. If I could do it all again, I would in a heartbeat. It didn't take long for me to settle into University life. I had just got my first car from my parents so I would drive up and down to university most days. The university had arranged a parking space for me near the door, so I did not have to do too much walking. In my first year my timetable was pretty full of a lot of classes most days. It was a combination of lectures and practical lab work. In between classes we would go to the canteen, wander round Dundee or dive into the pub for a pint. It just felt like a really easy way to live, we were just in first year and nothing was too difficult.

One of the feelings I clearly remember at that time was the joy of being back within mainstream educational expectations.

I had just spent from the age of 11 till the age of 20, in Special Education.

Much as they try to make it so, University is not the real world and it is a very sheltered, nurturing environment. I remember it just feeling so good to be on an expected life path. I had left the mainstream education system at the age of 11 because I wasn't coping with it. It was difficult because I couldn't keep up with it and I was being bullied. I did not like it. Of course, people were over 18 now and the name calling that took place in the playgrounds had all stopped.

Instead of being bullied I was included and made to feel welcome and it was absolutely amazing. Best of all about my days at university was that it was never assumed that I had learning difficulties. I never had to prove to anyone that I understood something. Nobody ever spoke slowly and deliberately to me or used hand signals in some inappropriate way to try and help me understand. I never had to prove anything to anybody, otherwise, I would not have been there. I loved it. It felt like shelter from the outside world. Shelter from the real world of bullies, or torments of having to prove my intelligence to everyone even down to the woman that sells me the newspaper in the morning. Just being a student at university was all people needed to know.

It was no mistake that I went to study Biotechnology. I loved biology and this is what I wanted to do. At that time, the early 1990's, Biotechnology was the most emerging and exciting field of science. I was excited to be studying it and I was thankful that I had discovered it at the time I had. This was a future field and I wanted to be part of it. The first years of the course were taken up with generic courses in physiology, chemistry, and biochemistry. I really enjoyed it and I didn't find it too difficult because I had studied A levels which are a little bit more advanced than the Scottish Higher. Things became much harder of course as time went on into 3rd and 4th years. But, I was content to just enjoy the early years while I could because I had a long uphill battle ahead of me.

The further I got into my degree the more and more difficult it became to keep up with my peers. Students today receive support but I believe that the provision for disabled or dyslexic students is still not great. Back then I received next to nothing in the form of support. I had extra time to write my exams but that was about it. I used to sit beside a great friend in class who would come with me to the library after class and allow me to photocopy her notes. This was the only help I received. I am hoping that disabled students going through university now are better supported than I was.

Things are very different for students now and life must be a bit easier. In the early 1990's there were no mobile phones, there was no internet and there was no Amazon!

If you wanted to read a book or a journal you had to go to the library, use whatever system they had to locate the book, then go to the shelf often to find it wasn't there at all. Now if you want a book you find it on Amazon, then, after a couple of clicks, it will drop through your letterbox at some point the next day. It is a different world now altogether. I cannot overstate how utterly EXHAUSTED I used to become at university trying to track down books and research papers.

The sheer effort of getting to the university, going up stairs and along corridors to the library, then up and down stairs within the library, I used to be physically weary before I could even start my studying.

It was really difficult and I found it very challenging. Sometimes when a lecture finished there was almost like a race to the library to see if you could get the right book because there were not enough copies to go around. It must be so different now, we have the World information at our fingertips and you don't have to leave your room. You probably don't even need to leave your bed to listen into a lecture now. You can probably download a podcast of it and listen to it on your phone. I have thought on many occasions how studying must be entirely different now and a lot less physically demanding. This would benefit me tremendously because I did have a really tough struggle at the time.

The further I got into my course, the more my late start in education might have been catching up with me and my dyslexia making things increasingly challenging. Reading lists grew longer, and the time we had to absorb information became shorter. Frustration was starting to show and I would become agitated if I thought I wasn't keeping up or understanding things. I can particularly remember in the later stages of the course having difficulties with laboratory work. Putting theory together with the practical work in the lab was challenging. I laboured on and had someone come to read things to me at times to try and get through the reading lists.

I was enjoying university life a lot and had made some great friends and I was involved with a couple of clubs and society. As soon as I arrived at university, one of the first clubs that I joined was the hillwalking club. I had just spent four years in Coventry in the centre of England where there were not a lot of open spaces and there certainly weren't any hills. There must have just been something within me at the time that loved nature and being outdoors. I now think that this is something that I've always had and maybe just didn't realise it at certain times. I really wanted to go up into the hills again as I had done with my family when I was a child. I remember meeting for the first time in the Student Union bar where they were planning the first trip of the year. They seemed happy for me to go along and see how I got on. I didn't know whether or not I'd be able to keep up with other people or go the distance, so I opted for the shortest walk on the day. The rain was lashing down from the moment we left Dundee until we got back again in the evening. It didn't stop us though. As we drove up the eastern glens the scenery became more and more beautiful as we travelled towards our destination, Glen Clova. There was another group going out to do a longer walk but I joined a group doing a walk called the Loop of Loch Brandy. Loch Brandy was not too far. I still remember being exposed to the elements and the feeling of space which I loved. This was a feeling that I would go onto crave as this just became the first of many walks that I did with the club and friends from the University. Over the winter months, when daylight was short, we would leave Dundee in the dark in order to get onto the hills and maximise the daylight we had. I really loved it and soon began to climb some of the Scottish mountains. It was around then, I learned what a Munro was. Named after the climber Hugh Munro, a Munro is a mountain over 3000ft or 900m high of which there are around 287 in Scotland. After the excitement of climbing my first Munro, it was amazing how one became two and I was soon ticking them off. By the time I had left university I had climbed around twenty five Munros. These were very happy times, I just loved being outdoors and being with nature and putting myself up against the elements. I loved the space and the challenge of it as well as the sense of achievement at the end of the day. It was where I was at my happiest. I became a lot fitter and ended up climbing some really quite challenging mountains. The effort it took was phenomenal!

When others were going out to climb three, four or more peaks in a day, I was happy to do one. The one I am most proud of climbing is a mountain in Glen Coe called *Bidean nam Bian.* It was an extremely challenging climb. I met a friend years later who had climbed it with me and he said, 'How on earth did we get you up there David?'

 I do not know how we did it, I must have been so committed and determined. I have driven past the mountain more recently and thought I would not go up there again. At the time I just loved it and thrived on the challenge.

My friends were really good with me, completely supportive and patient and completely understood the extra effort and phenomenal amount of energy that these sorts of activities took out of me. Not everybody was the same though, not everyone had the patience to wait for me or appreciated the extra effort it had taken me. But, I had some good friends who did and they were the people who counted the most. I had a lot of friends in the hall of residence and at the hillwalking club and I was just enjoying my life.

The later stages of the course were more difficult and I felt like I worked really hard. I used to go and work in the medical school library as I loved the atmosphere there. When I was a kid I always wanted to do medicine and be a doctor but gaining entry into medical school was a tall order for anyone. Given the late start I had I was just content to be studying at university at all. I don't know what it was inside me that gave me the drive and deep desire to go to university. I certainly never felt pressured by my parents and I wasn't doing anything for their benefit.

I remember at the time many people that I had known in the small town of Haddington had finished school and gone onto university.

It must have just felt like what people did in our middle-class bubble that we lived in.

I just wanted to be like everyone else and prove that I had the same ability as the next person.

I finished my degree in 1995 and ended up with a 2.2 honours degree. As my dad used to say, not bad for a so-called slow learner as I had been labelled all of my life. At the time I probably felt that I had worked so, so hard for it that I wanted a 2.1, however a 2.2 was fantastic and it opened doors for me to undertake further study and that is exactly what I did.

Chapter 5

I spent the summer of 1995 working on a farm just outside Haddington, just as I had every other summer since I started university. For some reason I was absolutely determined to work on a farm over the summer and through the harvest season. The whole of East Lothian has some of the best arable land in the country and it is prime wheat growing land. Haddington is surrounded by farms and has always had the feeling of a real country place. Growing up there was a joy and farms and countryside just become woven into the fabric of your being, as they did mine. Even to this day there is little I like more than the smell of fresh cut wheat in the summertime. So faced with the long summer ahead of me I was determined to work the harvest on a local farm.

I started answering adverts in the local newspaper, the East Lothian Courier and I had a couple of interviews but nothing came of any of them. Perhaps farmers were unsure of taking me on when farming was such physical work and I was an unknown. Nothing was forthcoming so I took matters into my own hands. I simply got into the car and started driving round farms until, after plenty of rejections, eventually I stopped at a farm close to where I lived and there was a man right there who turned out to be the farmer. We had a chat and he must have taken my phone number. Later that day he phoned and asked if I would come along the next morning, I was amazed but excited at the same time. That's how it happened, I worked for him the next four summers in a row. I was just so thrilled and grateful, and I still am, how this man was prepared to give me a chance. It wasn't all plain sailing, or plain farming, this was my first proper job and I had a lot to learn. I'm sure I used to drive him mad with my attitude at times. However, I loved being on the farm. I loved driving the tractor, taking loads off the combine on a summer's evening. There was something about that whole scene that felt really good and I still love it today.

During this time I had been applying for postgraduate courses. I knew by then that I hadn't got a 2.1 degree or better so going straight onto a PhD wasn't an option. If I wanted to try for a PhD, which I did, I would have to do a masters degree first. At that time there were two areas of study that interested me. Biomedical ethics was a growing area at the time and this had sprung up from the developments in

Biotechnology. Scientists were beginning to manipulate genes for example and ethical questions were springing up all over the place. I had an offer to go and study an MSc in Biomedical Ethics at University of Birmingham. The benefits of taking this course was that there were no practical elements to it. It was moving away from bench or laboratory science into a different area altogether, of ethics and philosophy. It would have been really interesting I have no doubt and I was genuinely interested in it. Moving away from science for me had the advantage that my manual dexterity, or lack of it, was not going to be an issue for me any longer. In the end, I followed my heart. I still really loved pure science and did not want to go in a different direction. I was offered a place at the University of Manchester, department of Medicine to study for an MSc in Cell & Molecular Biology in Human Disease. I was absolutely thrilled to have reached that level and been offered a place at an institution such as this was just amazing! Nobody ever thought I would study at that sort of level. It was a Massive Achievement!

I finished up on the farm after the harvest and started preparing for a new life in Manchester. I heard it was a big busy city but didn't know much about it at the time. I had been down for a brief interview with the course director but that was about all. I had to find myself somewhere to live for the duration of my course. By this time, it was well into the autumn and most places, university accommodation that is, were full and I was having difficulty finding a suitable place. I wanted to secure fully catered digs because I knew it would be a little bit easier for me if I didn't have to worry about practical living things like shopping and cooking. Time was wearing on however and I was struggling to find somewhere but eventually I found a bed in what seemed like an acceptable location.

At the beginning of October, I moved into a small hall of residence, just over a mile from the Medical School, called Luther King House. It was, as the name suggests, a Theological College that trained pastors from a number of denominations. The hall would fill up with theological students and any beds leftover were given out to those on other courses. Non ministry students were affectionately known as lay students. I moved in there and was probably one of around 20 lay students out of a population of just over 100. It was a small and really friendly place to be and it didn't take me long to make some really nice friends. When I first went to Manchester, knowing what a big and busy city it was, I decided not to take a car, but to use a bike instead.

Shortly before, I went I bought myself a brand new bike that was to do me for travelling around on. It was a mountain style bike with big chunky tyres, ideal for bumpy streets. They had secure lock ups for my bike at the halls. I started cycling backwards and forwards to university with my books on my back. I do remember that this was the first time I had really used a bike for travelling around a city and it was the first time I had come across segregated cycle lanes. I still remember cycling toward university and being amazed how the cycle lane left the road, turned into a park, and the little crossing there forced the traffic to stop and allowed bikes priority. This was 1995 and I just hadn't come across this concept before. For me cycling always had to be on busy roads so it was really fantastic to come across a different approach to cycling.

I thought Manchester was just amazing at the time, I hadn't seen anything like it. If anything, the sheer scale and business of the place was the thing that spooked me the most. The size of the medical school itself was bigger than the entire Abertay University. I had gone from a very sleepy little town to a huge major city and it took time to get used to it. I remember there was a lot of talk among people in the hall about crime and keeping yourself safe and certain areas of the city that might not be safe. It got on top of me for a while and I became very conscious of security. I have to say now that for the entire two years I was in Manchester I never felt unsafe and I did not encounter any hassle. I found the people very welcoming and friendly and I soon settled into the way of university life.

I felt amazing being a postgraduate student. It was just a thrill. I'm smiling as I type this thinking about how much it really meant to me at the time.

After all I had been through and all the people who wrote me off as having learning disabilities, I was at Manchester Medical School beginning my postgraduate degree!

A decade ago my parents had been fighting tooth and nail just to get me a chance at an education. They had received a letter to say I would never sit an exam and there was a day centre on the other side of town I could attend on leaving school.

I felt amazing just for being there finally at Manchester University.

My course was soon underway. There were only four of us on the course and I didn't have much of a timetable. I went into the university once or twice a week and the rest was up to me. I would live in the halls with other students or meet friends in the library. It was just a nice way of being and I was enjoying it very much. The hall or residence was great. I met some really nice friends there. After dinner we would study for a couple of hours then meet for coffee or go to the pub. Many of my friends at that time were studying theology or training to be pastors. We would have some great theological discussion over pints of an evening or sometimes over curry. I lived in the area of Manchester famous for its Curry Mile and used to love the food that was right on our doorsteps. With the hall being a theological college I soon settled into the routine of grace before dinner and evening prayers. Funny the little things that stick with you years on. Sometimes instead of saying grace we would sing a chorus of 'All Gods Gifts' and it would make the hair on the back of my neck stand up. I can still remember singing that very chorus as a 5 year old in the school halls of primary 1.

It's funny how, once the seeds of faith are established in you, they often never leave you, or indeed that's what happened to me. I had gone to church on and off through my teens but it was only once I got to Manchester that really understood and grasped faith. These two precious years had a huge influence on my spiritual life. I'm so thankful for the friends I made and the relationships I formed. As we will see later in the story, it took me longer to fully understand the importance of maintaining a spiritual life.

The Start of a Decline

It felt like everything had just come together for me and I was happy and enjoying my life. I felt really excited about the future. After my postgraduate course I could possibly go on to get a PhD or train for a job as a research assistant in the field that I loved. There was nothing not to like.

Yet one day, I can remember it like it was yesterday, I was cycling home from university through the park and suddenly I was aware of tears running down my face. I was upset, I was crying and I didn't know why.

Everything was great, life was better than I thought possible, but that unfortunately was the start of a long history of mental health difficulties. It was still early days in my course, I think it was the November after I had gone there when things went downhill. I started lying awake the entire night and feeling ill during the day. It wasn't long until someone suggested I go and see a doctor. I did this and the doctor put me on medication for depression.

How could I be depressed?

I was enjoying my life more than ever. I had some wonderful friends, a girlfriend, and I was enjoying university life yet I felt awful. I had never come across depression or thought about mental health before but it wasn't long before I realised what was happening to me. There was no explanation or any apparent reason for it then. Everything in my life seemed to be going swimmingly so why this big fall from health?

It didn't matter to me why at the time, I just wanted to get well and feel better again. I would be up and unable to sleep during the night-time but sleep during the day. I discovered the university counselling service and the chaplaincy centre where I would go for support. Unfortunately, things were not better by Christmas time and it was suggested that I pack up and go back to Scotland and even defer my course for a year. I wasn't going to university or keeping up with course work and the tutors knew I wasn't well. Yet, something inside wouldn't give in and wanted to keep pushing forward. My parents came to Manchester for the weekend ultimatum to take me back home until I was well again but I wouldn't go. The doctor had even suggested that I go home for a good while and get well. I don't know what it was that made me so, but I was determined to stay in Manchester, and I did.

Weeks went by and I continued to have support from a couple of places and I was on the road to recovery. Although I do remember it feeling like a very long road to get well again. I can't describe the pain that I felt inside. I did not feel able to explain it to anyone. I think it is like that with mental health, it is such a personal thing and very hard to describe accurately to others how you feel. After many months of unhappiness, I started slowly working back into my course and trying to catch up on coursework. The university must have been good about it because I don't remember them insisting I had to repeat anything. Before I knew it, I was into the second half of the course, a six months research project. I had connected with a department whose work didn't require too much manipulative laboratory work so this suited me very well. It was the Arthritis Research Unit who looked into genetic links to various diseases. I found it really challenging and I received valuable support. I really enjoyed it as much as I had enjoyed all of my studies up until then. I treated the research project, more or less, as a job. I would go into the labs or the office most days and work. I was actually disappointed afterwards when someone told me that I really didn't have to do that. I could have come and gone as I pleased. Hopefully it did me good and stood me in good stead for working life to come.

The Next Stage

It was soon time for me to leave university and the medical school behind and I started to look around for other things to do. My big plan was always to go all the whole way and do a PhD. This had been my ambition since I started university in 1991. I began by asking around the department but there was nothing, or all the studentship money for that year had already been allocated. I applied for many PhD studentships at other institutions but was unsuccessful. There weren't many of us on the course but the rest of them went straight onto PhD's. After a lot of searching, I ended up on a short term training scheme in a local research institute. This was 1997 and in those days the Labour government had invented the 'Training for work Scheme.' It was a six month placement where you worked full time as you trained but you weren't paid a salary. I visited the research institute, had a tour and interviews with various departments. They were all willing to take me on for six months so I had to decide which department or area of study I wanted to work in.

The department that most took my fancy at that time was called the Department of Epithelial Biology. They were investigating cancer in the large and small bowel. That was it, I was working in cancer research for the next six months and thought that was the start of my career.

I used to bounce into the labs on a Monday morning, or on any other morning for that matter. I loved what I was doing and loved being there. It was such interesting work, it didn't always feel like work and I was mixing with some really nice people. I liked the whole atmosphere at that time, people seemed to respect each other. This might have just been because I was just a trainee at the time, but people were really nice to me. I spent most of my time in the labs, doing write ups or reading up on research. I really enjoyed it and was so delighted that I was doing what I finally wanted to do.

It was getting near the end of my six month stay at the institute and I was starting to look around for jobs. For some reason, and I don't know why, I was keen to go back to Scotland at that time. So I started applying for jobs in and around Edinburgh and eventually got an interview with a Professor at the Western General Hospital in Edinburgh. The job would be carrying on working in cancer research, this time in Breast Cancer which I was delighted about. So in the summer of 1997. I packed up and left Manchester. I had developed a huge affection for Manchester and its people, I was absolutely blessed to meet so many great colleagues. I was keen however to be back in Edinburgh so I left. Unfortunately, I still regret leaving Manchester to this day. I didn't think for a single moment that I would never work in science again, but that was to be the outcome!

Chapter 6

In September 1997, I moved into a small flat in the west end of Edinburgh. It was a nice modern 1980's flat in a really quiet neighbourhood. It is funny the things you remember. I was moving my belongings from my parent's house to the flat on the afternoon of Princess Diana's funeral so the roads were very quiet. I bought this flat from my parents. When my dad had been really busy in his business they would use the flat during the week and go home to Haddington only at the weekend. I was very lucky to buy the flat from them because it was a way onto the property ladder for me. However, when I first moved in I began renting it from them in 1997 because I wasn't set up with a job. I had come back to Edinburgh thinking I was about to work at the WGH or with a similar job in research. I was continuing to apply for PhD studentships and despite having a couple of interviews, I wasn't getting very far. I remember one interview in particular that I was really enthusiastic about. It was at the University of Edinburgh working in Developmental Biology. I went along for an interview and was shown around and met the Professor. Everything seemed good and I was really into the subject. However, after a brief interview I was told that there would be a lot of fine dissection involved. The department didn't think I would have the motor skills to be able to carry out this work and, on that basis, I was turned down. This sort of activity would go on for the next few years. I had interview after interview, but I was never the right candidate. I had lots of interview skills training, did my best to try and articulate more clearly, but nothing happened. I used to worry that it was my verbal communication difficulties that were putting employers off because I had up to date skills. I was applying for jobs that maybe required a degree, knowing I had a postgraduate degree. I applied for positions as research assistant or research technician as well as many more PhD studentships. I had countless interviews in all sorts of places but I was never the successful candidate. I would always ask for feedback which I began to be able to predict. I was always a great candidate with great skills, but someone else always had the edge and was offered the position.

I was still keen to keep up my skills in cancer research so I managed to arrange some training similar to the set up I had been on in Manchester. It was a training for work scheme this time for three months in a Breast Cancer unit of the WGH. Again, I enjoyed this placement very much although at the end of it I was told there was no money available to employ me. At the same time as I was working there, there was another trainee. But she was still a student finishing off her undergraduate degree. I had made a good friend with someone who worked there. We started riding our bikes together. Much later I realised that the professor had managed to find the money to employ this less qualified person but not me! It didn't matter that I was more highly qualified and had far more skills yet, there was nothing available for me.

This was the moment - the first time in my life I had ever uttered the words or even thought about Disability Discrimination.

I was beginning to put things together in my head and maybe, or maybe not, come up with the right answer. How could it be that, to the best of my knowledge, all my contemporaries from my MSc course had gone on to further study. To the best of my knowledge all my friends from Dundee had gone onto jobs or further study. I thought about the interview at Edinburgh University and being turned down because I wasn't able to carry out fine dissections. I thought about the countless interviews I had where I had been told I was a great candidate, just never good enough to obtain the job.

Months slipped into years and the time I had been out of science just became longer and longer and made it much more difficult for me to get back in. Up to date skills in science can become outdated very quickly. I faced an even bigger struggle to get back into the work. Throughout all this time my mental health started to deteriorate again. Long term unemployment does that to you. You lose your self-esteem, sense of purpose or worth and things, for me anyway, went rapidly downhill. The local hotel bar became the centre of my social life while drinking was the thing that took up most of my time. Drinking became problematic at that time too. With little motivation and feeling defeated I spent a lot of time drinking. I was fine for a while but eventually started to get in trouble with the Police through drink and did a few things I'm quite ashamed of.

After much unhappiness I eventually got an opportunity. Through a contact of a friend I found a job in an electronics factory. I was spending my days opening mail and filing things into alphabetical order. I felt so degraded and undervalued, I just hated it. After a year of this, I was still filing and doing menial tasks. I was still drinking heavily and was deeply unhappy. I got myself dismissed from this job in quite an undignified manner and before long I was back on the dole again.

This turned out to be the first in a series of really awful jobs that I tried but didn't manage to hold down.

It felt like society has very low expectations or belief in disabled people.

I spent the next few years going around disability employment agencies trying to get support to get into work. There are numerous agencies set up to help disabled people into work.

However, they seem to have very low expectations of disabled people. Sure enough they could help me work in retail, catering or security say, but anything more cerebral they had no clue. As for my field of Molecular Biology, they didn't even know what that was.

They would offer to help me complete application forms, but my written English was usually better than theirs. Disability charities, particularly disability employment charities, became one of my bugbears. Keen to talk about disability employment but never willing to employ disabled people themselves. I continued to apply for jobs but with little success. I have had some really awful jobs, often accompanied by some pretty grim awful people. When I did find a job I would make it work for a while then I usually became frustrated and angry and would find myself ejected.

By this time in my life I had begun to find outlets for my frustrations and ways of being creative, and one of these was through writing. I tried my hand at creative writing and I tried to become a journalist. I found writing really therapeutic and I still do. I began writing about my experience and sending it in to newspaper editors. To my amazement I started receiving emails back from journalists saying that my work had been accepted and they were going to publish it in the newspapers. Before I knew it, I had photographers in my front room taking photos of me and I was in the national papers the next day. I started submitting more and more pieces and they continued to be accepted. I was in contact with a couple of disability organisations and started receiving calls from their media department. I remember a call from Leonard Cheshire at 1pm one afternoon asking me if I would mind being interviewed for Sky News. By 5pm that evening I had a film crew in my front room interviewing me. It really felt surreal. This went on for a few months and I started to write commissions from a couple of papers. I then started writing frequently for online magazines and journals which led me to set up my own website and blog. I started writing and blogging all about disability, about benefits and disability politics. It was all fine for a while but looking back, it wasn't making me happy. It wasn't the thing that I wanted to be doing and it was not being a true part of who I was.

The Turning Point

I have tried to articulate to you in these pages the utter frustration I have felt over the years. Knowing how hard my parents fought to get me a chance at an education in the first place, and just how hard I had worked to achieve my degrees. Never in my wildest dreams would I have imagined how difficult it would be to get work.

I can't say for sure what has caused my mental health difficulties over the years, but I know this serious challenge has not helped.

The constant feelings of rejection, of not feeling good enough and having little sense of self-worth. Some things stick with you for years.

The hurt, the rejection, the emptiness, it all catches up with you in the end. That's exactly what happened and things came to a head in 2014. I can easily say that was the worst time in my life. I don't know how you define a breakdown, but I would guess that was as awful as I ever want to experience. I was deeply unhappy and had some personal problems that I just didn't see a way out of. Sometimes, when you are in the depths of despair you cannot see a way out. I was in the middle of my life and I felt as if I had not much to show for it. I had been unemployed for years, was living alone, and I really did not see a future for myself. I was in the depths of despair the lowest I had ever been. I will never forget watching the opening ceremony of the Glasgow 2014 Commonwealth Games. This was a wonderful, beautiful spectacle of sport, but I felt so ill, so broken and so unhappy at the time. I felt that there was no hope, no light at the end of the tunnel. I couldn't see a happy and fulfilling future for myself. I was in the darkest place for what felt like an eternity. It felt like it went on for months and there was no light at the end of the tunnel.

There was a way out however, and of course things slowly improved. Through long term therapy and the support of some close friends, I began to rebuild my life. It was the start of a very long road clawing my way back to good health.

Chapter 7

Lives can change and things turn around pretty quickly indeed. I had been really ill for a few months and was sick and tired of feeling low. It had been a great summer, I remember lots of good weather but I felt like I'd missed it all. I had been so low and so stuck in my own thinking that it had just passed me by. This seemed to go on for a long time until one morning I bumped into someone I hadn't seen for a while and didn't really know well at that time. Normally when anyone asks how you're feeling you say 'great, fine' but I didn't that morning, I said I felt awful and things weren't good. Having the courage to say that felt like a big thing. We try to put on a brave face, we try to show the world we are strong and in control but often we're not. We try to make out we are having a good time, but on the inside feel awful. I am writing this chapter towards the end of May 2019. In the last few weeks there have been a super series of programs on BBC television about Mental Health. High profile celebrities, football players and household names have been on prime time television talking about their experiences of mental health. It is really great to see. I find it very reassuring to see people in what I consider privileged positions struggling with exactly the same issues as me. Mental Health doesn't discriminate on the grounds of wealth, or alleged success, it affects everyone no matter what your background. But tragically it has taken long enough before Mental Health has come out into the open and people are talking about it the way they are now. It was still difficult in 2014 to tell people you were suffering with Mental Ill Health. Back in 1995 when I first fell seriously ill, I actively tried to hide it.

The Start of My Recovery

It can be the most simple of things that can literally turn your life around, some words, a saying, or an image. For me, it was finding the thing, whatever it was, that could make me happy again. It sounds so simple now but when you are in the depths of despair and depression, it is not that simple you cannot see a way out. You are side blinded. You cannot believe you will ever be happy again. It is not simply resolved and it wasn't at the time, but it was a start. I began a very long course of therapy with a suitably qualified person and engaged on a long journey of self-discovery.

I spent the rest of the summer, riding my bike and digging my allotment. I would like to remind everybody of the beneficial effects of exercise and fresh air. I have had an allotment for around seven years and I really think it has literally saved my life at times. When I have been in the depths of depression and despair I have gone there simply just to be. That is what I did in 2014 when I was so unwell, I used to go to the allotment Just To Be ! It didn't matter if I did any work or just sat in the shed and read a book. There was something soothing about just being there and being surrounded by the healing effects of nature. I would go to the allotment and, whatever was on my mind was still there, but being in that environment seemed to help me process this and feel just a tiny bit better.

I achieved a similar effect when I was riding out on my bike. Although I lived in central Edinburgh, within 20 minutes cycling I reached some quiet country roads. Edinburgh is a great place to be a recreational cyclist. Whilst having the benefits of living in the city there are countless lovely routes to be found not far outside the city. It is difficult to overestimate the benefits of being outdoors and exercising and that is what I did. Importantly, I simply continued to do it. It felt like taking my hands off the controls of life and just letting go. I love the analogy of a light aircraft spinning out of control when the pilot switches on the radio and shouts 'Mayday

Mayday.' Someone gets back to her and shouts, 'take your hands off the controls' and after a while reluctantly she does and the plane rights itself and she regains control. I think our lives are a bit like that, we try to take charge of everything and manipulate things our way. We become frustrated and cross when events do not materialise as we would wish.

Letting go can be terrifying but when we do we realise that we don't need to control things, life happens by itself. By freeing ourselves up like this we can find increasingly more energy to focus on the things that make us feel happy and feel healthy.

At that time it felt incredibly like the first time I had really begun to accept my situation. Most of my efforts up until then, had been done with a view to acquiring a job, or bettering myself in some way. I had completed countless training courses and volunteered in many placements because I thought it might help me obtain work or make money or start a career.

Now I was living my life and spending my time doing things for no other reason or motive than that they made me feel happy. It was like a massive weight off my shoulders and I was making strides back to improving my health and well-being,

I think it is important to also acknowledge at this point that I was becoming well again in large part as a result of therapy. Over the years, Counselling and Psychotherapy have been an integral part of my recovery. Talking Therapy on the whole is good as long as you ensure you are working with suitably qualified and skilled people. I was very lucky because I came into contact with someone who was extremely talented. This person really helped me enormously.

I continued simply being and doing what made me feel good for a long time. I think that was an important factor, that I maintained this. I am sure many of us do things for a while to try, or see how it is, and things come and go. We either do things for a reason, a season or for life. When we find the things that really connect with us, it usually naturally becomes something we do for life. Chatting with a friend recently he stopped and said to me 'I love how you just try everything David,' and he is right. I have tried a lot of different things. There has always been something within me that has made me want to try everything. I'm still the same. I want to experience more and more activities. I remember my parents telling me that when I was little, they would visit a clinic with me to let the paediatricians check up on my development. They told me that the doctors told my parents they must let me try anything and if I fall over then so be it. I think that attitude must have stuck with me all of my life because I have tried so many different challenges.

Amongst the scariest must have been rock climbing. I joined a climbing club in Edinburgh not long after I came back here to live in 1997. It went well for a while because over the winter people would practice on an indoor climbing wall. I really enjoyed working on strength and balance and it was good fun. Difficulties began when the weather got better and people began to want to climb outdoors. I went once or twice and really enjoyed it but, of course there were limits to what I could do. It became really difficult to find people patient enough to go out walking or climbing with me. Perhaps climbing wasn't the best thing I've ever tried but I did enjoy it. What all this has taught me, and what I did to get well again, was to do my own thing, whatever it took to make me happy. I continued doing it and grew stronger and healthier.

Reconnecting With Myself

By spending time outdoors again, riding my bike and being around nature, it soon became clear that this was the environment that I felt best in. I just wanted to be outdoors all the time, it was like a huge part of myself that I had either forgotten about or didn't realise. It felt like I had gone full circle right back to my childhood where I would spend long days outdoors either in the hills with my family or or just playing on the beach. It was where I was happiest and where I wanted to stay. Outdoor sport just became a bigger and bigger thing in my life. I never realised until then just what a large part of me it was, but here is a piece of an insight into how it happened.

Cycling

I cannot remember a time in my life, apart from a few years while I was in university, when I didn't have access to a bicycle. From my very first trike until today, bikes have always been in my life. Although I've not always been able to cycle the way I can now, it is training and commitment that has enabled me to do that.

I was about to go on holiday in 2006 and wanted to be fit and well for my trip and thought riding the bike would help. I started with really small runs round the block and really enjoyed it. After a while I began to want more so I joined a local club. This was one of the best things I ever did. One of the local cycling clubs in particular was very welcoming and supportive of me. I would start off with a short run and maybe catch a train back to Edinburgh. As I got stronger and fitter, I increased my stamina and I could cycle longer and further. A typical cycle started off as 10 miles, then it became 15, 20 miles as it gradually increased. Now I think nothing of cycling 30 -40 miles in a day. I find that a comfortable amount for me. Some people can do a lot more in a day but that is what feels good for me and suits my condition.

Knowing your limits is really important, but at the same time being able to push yourself a bit further is equally beneficial. It really intrigues me how many people I meet who, for whatever reason, have never ridden a bike. Often people tell me they could never ride a bike or cycle that sort of distance in a day. Absolutely sure enough, but, if they tell themselves or decide they could never do that, then they won't. However, that line of thought is every bit as absurd as thinking that I jumped out of bed one day and decided to travel on a 30 to 40 mile bike ride. It is ridiculous and should be seen for what it is. I started riding 5 miles, then 5miles became 10 miles and so on. Now, years later, yes, I can cycle 30 to 40 miles comfortably. But, like most other things that are worth doing, you have to work at it. Cycling is probably the Sport that I have stuck at and put the most effort into which is why I can cycle as I can.

It has not all been plain sailing, or plain cycling, there have been aspects of it that have caused me enormous frustration. I have to say a special thank you to the 'Road Club Edinburgh'.I joined the Road Club some years after the CTC because I wanted to try and take my cycling to the next level. While Cycling UK are focused on cycle touring, the road Club are more focused on cycle racing. At the time I joined I had no intention of ever racing on a bike if nothing else for the simple reason I was too scared! I was a big scaredy cat when going really fast on descending hills so there was no way I wanted to race. My focus was simply to become a stronger and fitter cyclist. I didn't know how far I could go but the important thing was learning to train for cycling.

I made some super friends in the Road Club who started spending a lot of time with me and they taught me a lot of excellent techniques. I started working hard at it and my cycling grew from strength to strength. It was amazing and I felt great. I started going to spin classes and spending more and more time in the saddle. It was fantastic.

Most people were really supportive. Unfortunately others were not!

This is something I have experienced in all sorts of mainstream sports clubs.

Often people think that if you look able-bodied, then you must be, or must be able to perform at the same level. However, it is not as simple as that and people need to be forgiven for their ignorance. I was constantly coming across people in the club who would say, 'Come on David, put the effort in, you don't try hard enough,' or, 'You don't want it enough.' I used to experience phenomenal pain while I was cycling. But to some, and it was the minority, their attitude was that, 'We all have pain, get over it.'

To compare an able-bodied person with someone like myself with CP was just ridiculous! You come across these people in every sphere of life who do not have the understanding or the intellect to grasp it. We should never be put off by them or be perturbed by their warped thinking but it is really tough, upsetting and devastating. For every one of these people, there are ten great people who care, understand and have the open mindedness to accept. I was lucky and found some great people.

My cycling continued to go from strength to strength and the next was to try racing. At the time there was a para-cycling race being staged just outside Edinburgh. I trained hard for it and did race just once. The key word being 'once.' I found it really difficult, and it was more pain that I was prepared to tolerate. I didn't want to try it again.

One branch of cycling that really enthralled me was track cycling. In 2014 the city of Glasgow hosted the Commonwealth Games and, in order to do this, Glasgow built a brand new velodrome. named after Sir Chris Hoy, our greatest British Olympian. After the games it was opened to the public. The first time I went to the Sir Chris Hoy Velodrome, I got on a track bike and immediately fell off before I was even near the track. This is a quite different style of cycling and it would take practice. Once I found my balance on the track I began to really enjoy it. I can't explain how much of a thrill riding the track was, you get a real rush of adrenalin coming round the banking. One thing led to another and I eventually got a trial for the British Paralympic Team. I was not picked for the team but it didn't upset me at all, I was just really proud to have achieved that level of cycling.

My achievements in cycling are possibly one of

the things I feel most proud of. I don't think anybody when I was younger would have ever envisaged me being able to ride a bike to the extent I have done and continue to do now. I am proud. I don't train the way I did a few years ago so inevitably I'm not as strong a cyclist as I was then, but I enjoy my cycling just as much as ever. Having been through that and had the training discipline as I did for a few years, I feel it has really paid off. It's a great lesson in applying yourself enough to something if you really want it. It is a choice, it is a decision. If you decide, as I suspect the majority of people do, that you will never ride a bike then you probably will not. People have to understand it is a choice. Whether it be riding a bike, or walking or any sort of activity, we can choose how we spend our time.

I think back to the absurdity of the people telling me they could never cycle the way I can, or as far as I can. It is always able-bodied people who say it to me.

Who is the disabled person now and what is disabling them?

Skiing

One of the best choices I ever made was to learn to ski. If ever there were a list of the most unlikely things I would ever do, skiing must have been top of the list. It makes me smile when I think back to the days in Scouts when we would go off to Glenshee for the day. The very notion of me going along with them would have been just absurd. But it was in Glenshee that I first put skis on my feet and promptly fell over. I think it was around 2000 or 2001 when a friend invited me up to Glenshee for the day. My first answer was no, and I told him that I'd never been skiing and it was very unlikely that I would have balance to be able to do it. My friend persisted and persuaded me to go up with him and just enjoy the mountains in the snow. That's how it happened. I spent the whole day rolling around in the snow but I had such a wonderful time. I made a few other day trips with him that winter and was absolutely hooked by then.

We are very lucky here in Edinburgh, we have the largest dry ski slope in Europe here, and funnily enough I can see it from my front window now. I made enquiries there, perhaps around the year 2001, as to whether or not I could have lessons or not. To my delight I found a group called 'The Uphill Ski Club.' It was a group that supported disabled people in learning to ski. I started going along there to weekly sessions. It was really difficult in the early days, I could hardly stand up in my ski boots let alone ski. Like everyone else I started on the nursery slopes where you carried your skis up to the top to spend five seconds sliding, or in my case, falling back down to the bottom. The physical energy it took just to do this was just phenomenal. In the early days I found that just putting ski boots on and trying to move in them was extremely tiring. Of course, I was falling all over the place at the time and discovering the mat was not soft like snow. It was hard and you could really hurt yourself on it. The entire rigmarole of falling over, trying to stand up and get back into my skis was just exhausting and the energy it took out of me is hard to describe.

So draining.

It wasn't enough to put me off, I was ' Motivated to Succeed.'

There was an army of volunteers connected with the club who turned up every week to support us and believe me I really needed the support. As time went on, I developed a particular friendship with a chap called Derek. Derek was retired and lived locally and we started meeting out-with club times to ski together. He spent hours and hours with me teaching me to ski. He was a real inspiration to me. A couple of years went by and I continued to practice my skiing. I would come home black and blue with bruises after falling on the mat. One day I even ended up in A&E to have stitches in my elbow after the matting had torn through my jacket and I had cut myself. Again, it still wasn't enough to put me off. I wanted to be able to ski and enjoy the mountains in the snow so much, there was a real steely determination. Derek would make a couple of trips to The Alps every year and come back and tell me all about it. Derek loved Courchevel and had been there so many times. He would tell me all about it and how the long gentle runs into the village would be ideal for the likes of me.

The hours of practice we spent on the dry slope began to pay off, and eventually I found my balance on the skis. It is difficult to explain but it was almost like a light bulb moment. I had spent so long falling all over the place and sometimes hurting myself, then suddenly it happened. I found my balance and all just fell into place. We made a few trips in a season to the ski stations in Scotland and I was really enjoying skiing. As time passed, my skiing capabilities improved so much that I wanted more, I wanted to ski 'The Alps.'

I set my heart on going to France to ski, but I had to work out the best way to make that happen. Yes, I was skiing by then but I still needed a lot of support with the logistics of skiing. I still found getting into my boots, walking in ski boots and carrying my skies really difficult. Often by the time I actually got onto the slopes and clipped into my skis, I would be exhausted before I even started. I needed support, someone to just be there to help lug my skies about or give me an arm back up when I fell, or even an arm to hold onto in the lift queue. So, I put my thinking cap on and started looking. I was buying ski magazines a lot at that time which put me even more in the mood. I loved the glossy pictures of snow-covered mountains and powdered snow being thrown up in the air like fairy dust. I would read all about the various resorts I'd never heard of, the number of lifts they had, the numbers of beginners runs. I would study their piste maps and imagine which way I wanted to go. I was pretty obsessed. I was desperate to go skiing.

One day, while flicking through a magazine I found myself looking at the small ads. One particular advert for a chalet company caught my eye. It was a company based in The Three Valleys in France, providing catered chalet holidays and, to my amazement, their address was somewhere just outside Edinburgh. I opened up my computer and sent them an email explaining that I would like to come out to France skiing and that I needed a little support and if this might be possible was this something they could provide. It just so happened that they were in Scotland at the time and they got right back to me and we arranged to meet for coffee in the cafe at the end of my street. We had a really nice chat and I explained the sort of support I need and they could not have been more positive and helpful and they said by all means come out and have a go.

I had a fantastic trip to Meribel in 'The Three Valleys' that winter. I spent a lot of time falling over in the snow but had a wonderful time. I didn't know how well I would be able to get around the mountain and even if I would travel out of the Meribel Valley. We spent the first few days not going far at all, practising on beginner's runs. We would go round an easy run, in and out of the trees. I was loving it and having so much fun. Then time came to go further afield and we decided to try going to the next valley over. So we travelled on a lift which felt really long to me at that time and eventually we reached the top of the next beautiful mountain. We climbed out of the lift and skied over a short plateau.

Suddenly I saw a huge brightly coloured sign. The sign said 'Welcome to Courchevel.' That moment will stay with me forever. I thought about Derek, and the hours and hours we had spent together on the dry ski slope. It felt like all the years of determination at being able to ski had paid off. I had wanted to be able to ski so much I was absolutely determined. Derek had taught me and encouraged me and he had told me so much about Courchevel.

Everything had led to this moment.

Since then I have made numerous trips to the 'The Alps' to ski. I have had wonderful times in 'The Three Valleys ' with people who, after meeting in the cafe, many years ago now have become dear friends of mine. I have now skied in a few different places in France, I've skied in Austria and in Andorra in the Pyrenees. Without a doubt, skiing is the thing that I love the most. If I could choose to do one thing for the rest of my days, I would spend it in the mountains skiing.

It is one of the few things that I do now where I don't feel disabled or at a disadvantage at all. When I have skis on and climb off the chair lift, I forget about everything, and most of all, I forget about disability.

I feel as able as the next person. The sense of freedom

and fulfilment I get from skiing I do not achieve from any other activity.

I have not found another place where I feel so free, so alive and so equal.

It is interesting that the activity I find most fulfilling and the place where I feel most alive, and the thing I like to do the most, is at the one I had to work hardest to achieve. There were no shortcuts to learning to ski. If there had been, believe me, I would have found them. It was something I wanted so much that I was determined to do whatever it took. What could we achieve if we applied the same determination to other areas of our lives? As a general rule, things really worth having, don't come easily. Some people are lucky, but the majority of us have to work at things to achieve our goals. Being able to ski was my goal. I was prepared to put in the months and years of practice in order to get it, and eventually I did. I am so grateful that I did, and I feel fantastic about it.

Sadly, Derek is no longer with us but I always think about him when I am skiing as I enjoy the gift of freedom that skiing brings so very much.

Chapter 8

Some of the best advice someone gave me is to do what makes you happy and just keep doing it. Up until then, whatever I had done, I did because I thought it might lead to a job, or help make money or further my contacts. I had never done anything that I did for no other reason but I enjoyed doing it, and it made me happy. This was all to change though. By this time I was well on my road to recovery and feeling better about myself and more positive about the future. I can't over emphasise the effect that doing sport had on me. I was riding my bike ridiculous amounts of miles and spending long days on the allotment in summertime. I couldn't wait for the winter though, skiing was everything and all I really wanted to do.

Spending so much time outdoors turned out to be a real wake up call to me, it was the place most alive, most happy and most content. I just wanted to be outside surrounded by nature. By this time I had been writing a blog for 3 years. I still enjoyed journalism writing and, although I wasn't getting paid to do it, I tried to keep my hand in by writing a blog. I wrote mostly about politics, particularly about disability rights, and wrongs. There had been huge changes in the welfare state in recent years and I wrote a lot about that. I was becoming quite jaded about it as well. I was writing about things I had absolutely no control over and thought that all the ranting wasn't changing anything. The truth was however, I was phenomenally bored with my writing and I must have been boring my readers at the same time. So the obvious thing to do was to start writing about what made me happy, and that was outdoor sports. That was the turning point and the start of something that would turn my life around.

Start of My Adventures

Earlier that year, coincidentally or not, I had met a friend who was planning a camping trip up to the north of Scotland. I had wanted to go up north for a long time but, for whatever reason, did not take the notion of going on my own. So, I asked if I could go too and she agreed. There was only one problem, she had just bought a new tent and was planning to camp. I hadn't been camping since my days in scout camp over 25 years previous. I thought camping was something you did when you were either young or broke. Why would anybody choose to go and camp knowing how unpredictable the Scottish weather was? I hadn't known her for very long and I wanted to prove that I was tough and up for anything, so I agreed to go.

We drove up to Ullapool for the first night's camp. Ullapool was 4 or 5 hours drive away so there was no running back home if I didn't like it. There had been nothing to worry about or not to like. Before long we were sitting in our seats eating a nice meal watching the ferries come to go up Loch Broom. It was beautiful and nothing else seemed to matter at that moment. Our night away turned into a four day trip which included taking in Durness right up on the north west coast of Scotland. We visited Cape Wrath, the most north westerly point on the British mainland. The journey from Ullapool up the west coast to Durness is difficult to capture in words. The mountains are spectacular and its a place of outstanding rugged beauty. The whole trip just reminded me how much I wanted to be in that environment and what it did for my well-being. I felt free, I felt alive, and I found contentment and that was everything.

We camped again later in the summer at a lovely spot in the Scottish Borders. The Etteric Valley was our next stop which, enhanced by fantastic weather, just reaffirmed to myself that this is what I wanted to do.

When I got back from that trip to the Borders, I updated my blog to say what a nice trip I had and suddenly were taking an interest in my blog. I was writing about something that made me feel good, I was excited about and that must have come across to my readers. It became really obvious to me then to do more, and I was beginning to think I have finally found my niche and my purpose.

My First Big Adventure

At that time I was doing a lot of cycling for myself as well as volunteering with an East Lothian charity. Cycling was my passion at that time so I was helping a group in Haddington who help provide cycling opportunities for disabled people. Before I came across this group, I had no idea of the range of bikes that were available to enable disabled people to experience the benefits of cycling. Huge trikes, side by side, and even a bike with a roll on platform for wheelchair users to get the benefits of being on a bike. I was really at home in that group and enjoyed helping out.

I was still cycling pretty hard myself at that time and still trying to keep up with the Edinburgh Road Club. Still trying to prove something to them, or to myself that I was as able as them to be 'accepted' into their group so to speak. The next step I thought was to set myself a challenge which still remains as one of the biggest physical achievements of mine and that is to cycle the Hebridean Way.

In September of 2016 we set off to cycle the Hebridean was, I on the bike and Eileen driving the car with all the kit in it. It was around the Autumn Equinox and the seas were pretty stormy and so one of the first things I remember was the ferry from Oban was delayed due to bad weather. Not a good start. Before then I had always considered myself a good sailor who didn't get seasick, but that crossing was when my opinion changed. I remember being distinctly unwell on the boat as there was a sizable swell particularly after we got out of the Sound of Mull and into the Atlantic. I tried to sleep or rest as well as I could in order to pass the time. It was dark by the time we arrived in Castlebay and fortunately that we had booked was almost and the other end of the ferry terminal. It was after 11pm when we got there and we more or less fell into bed.

I'll never forget waking up that morning to the sun flooding into the room and the moment I first looked out the window. To see Castlebay in the early morn, the sea very calm and Kisimal Castle out in the bay was just idyllic. I felt so excited that we were finally there and that morning I was about to begin my journey cycling the length of the Outer Hebrides. I had no idea what lay ahead of me but just felt excitement and wanted to get going. After breakfast the car was all packed up and ready to go and I was standing there with my bike. It felt strange that Eileen was getting ready to drive off in the car when I just had my bike. I had 185 miles ahead of me before I would travel in the car with her again.

At this point in my book I thought I'd include some extracts from my blog. I started writing about my adventures in 2016. As well as it being a great way to record my travels, I really enjoy writing about them and sharing it with other people. Following is an extract from my blog documenting my cycle up the Hebridean Way.

I was all packed and ready to go the night before when I received a text message from CalMac to say that the ferry was going to be delayed due to bad weather and that they would message again in the morning with an estimated time of departure. There had been a terrible storm over the weekend apparently and many of the sailings to the outer isles had been delayed. Could I have picked the worst possible week of the year to cycle the Outer Hebrides I asked myself, or was the storm about to pass and the weather to settle for the next few days? It made me think of the Clint Eastwood film where he points a six barreled gun with only one bullet to someone's head and asked, "Do you feel lucky?"
I hardly slept at all that night, not sure if it was because I was excited or just wondering if God would be kind after all and send

us the sunshine! We left Edinburgh sharp in case the ferry sailed on time, but shortly after we received a message to say it would at 4.30pm. By the time we got to Oban we had a couple of hours to kill. Oban is one of the few places where I ever miss, or think about, the Woolworth store. I've spent one too many rainy afternoons in Oban where we have dived into Woolworths to avoid being soaked and purchased something completely unnecessary to take back to the accommodation and never read.

The ferry eventually sailed at 5.30 after what felt like an eternity waiting in the car at the terminal. It was still lashing with rain at this point and it really felt like I was on a trip, sitting in a steamed up car listening to the rain. The first couple of hours on the journey were fine but as we got further out into the Atlantic the swell got up and after a plate of CalMac's finest Macaroni Cheese and chips, the meal of champions, I started to feel distinctly queasy. I felt reassured that I was not the only one as there was woman sitting nearby who looked very white about the gills and couldn't sit for more than five minutes without going for a walk. I managed a bit of sleep however and before I knew it I could see the lights of Kisimul Castle and at 11pm, a bit bleary eyed, arrived at our Hostel.

As soon as we arrived at Dunard Hostel on Barra, I wanted to write about it straight away. It felt decidedly quirky with its multi colour décor and 70's wood panelling up the stairs. It looked from the outside a bit dilapidated and the inside, well perhaps we could describe it as rustic. I didn't really care about anything, I was so exhausted and just wanted to get to bed, I would have slept anywhere.

I had a really good nights sleep and I even slept through all the announcements and noise of the 7am ferry leaving from across the road. Then, I had a magical moment, I got up, looked out of the window and got my first glimpses of Castlebay on the beautiful isle of Barra. The sun was out, there wasn't a breath of wind and the sea looked like a sheet of glass. A small medieval castle called Kisimul Castle stood right in the centre of the bay. It looked majestic. It was a special moment because I had no idea what was there. It had been completely dark when we arrived late the night before. I felt so excited and couldn't wait to get on the bike that day to start my journey.

The first day on my Cycling adventure Barra to South Uist

We had a comfortable enough sleep in the Dunard hostel that night although I was so shattered after the journey to get there I would have slept anywhere. The beds were a bit rickety and the mattress really soft so not recommended for a prolonged stay. The décor in the front room was a kind of terracotta and blue in the style of a pseudo Mediterranean theme. The hostel itself was inexpensive, functional and did the trick. My only regret was that the staff were not very cheerful and I did not manage to get a smile or a welcome word out of them!

When it comes to accessibility, it is not suitable for disabled people. The hostel reminded me of an old fisherman's house with a steep set of well worn concrete steps leading up to the front. There was no hand rail and I could not even carry my own bag up the steps!

The first task of the day was to cycle down to the island of Vatersay where The Obelisk marks the start of the Hebridean Cycle Way. It was a little further away than I thought and involved two hills round a couple of bays. As soon as I left Castlebay there was really quite a steep climb which gave me a bit of a fright! I'm not sure what I was expecting but I had in my mind gentle rolling hills for the first few days and I wasn't even out of Castlebay. This gave my lungs a sharp wake up. For a minute or two I wondered if I was really up for this adventure as it was a really steep hill!

My first brief stop to admire the first of two war memorials I would see on my short run done to Vatersay. Perched on the top of the hill looking over castle bay was a three-sided monument at a beautiful, sculpted angels on the top of each corner, the sides bearing the names of the people who fell in the war. Four flag poles stood behind and a few wind battered wreaths lay strewn at the bottom. I loved the contemporary feel of which shows that the memories of the world wars and thankfully not fading, and that remembrance is still part of our psyche today. Further round towards Vatersay, was another memorial beside the wing of a war plane that have come down. Unfortunately, I didn't stop at this one but would be well worth it I imagine.

When I got to the start of the Hebridean Way, I had in my mind a great big monument towering into the sky and partially blocking out the sunlight. To my surprise there stood a gate behind which was a footpath leading to the starting post. A post it was, certainly no bigger that and from the road I had to strain my eyes to see it. I didn't want to walk up the hill to it and leave the bike by the road, nor did I want to risk cycling over to it and risk a puncture twenty minutes into my adventure, so I stood with my back it and had my photograph taken. Now people can see the photograph and play spot the Obelisk in the background as it really is quite a challenge.

As soon as I left Vatersay, I really felt good because I had finally arrived at the start of my Amazing Adventure and I was beginning my tough special long distance cycle journey of 185 miles from Barra to Butt at last. After all the planning and thinking and packing I had finally arrived and I felt great. So I did what I thought every Adventurer does at the start of their expeditions, brimming with confidence, I stopped and had a banana. The sun was shining brightly and the sky was opaline blue. Barra was looking stunning and I sat and took it all in for a little while. It felt such an exquisite special moment which I had been waiting for a while to come- just Me, the Bike, the Hebrides.

Barra is really small and it didn't take me long to cycle up the West Coast and across the island to Ardhmor to catch the ferry to Eriskay. In the North west of Barra we spotted a sign for the airport and, with time to kill before the ferry,

I decided to check out the facilities there. I cycled the mile long road into the Airport that ran along the side of the most beautiful white sandy beach which actually turned out to be the runway. Barra airport is one of few in the world where planes land on the beach so arrivals and departures were subjected to tidal times! We went into the cafe at the airport for something to eat. I use the word cafe here because it was, but at the same time it doubled up as, check-in hall, departure lounge, arrivals hall and observation room! Yes, Barra airport consists of about one room with a desk in one corner and a fridge in the other. I didn't see any sign of security! Perhaps it did happen out of sight but when the plane was about to depart to other shores, a man came into the cafe and shouted, 'Anymore for Glasgow?' and that was it. It really made me laugh inside thinking about all the issues we have at International airports with check-in and security. How civilised I thought, being able just to turn up, chuck your bag in the trolley and get onto the plane, I'm sure they'd let you take chips on with you if you hadn't finished them before you had to go. You certainly wouldn't get a bottle of spring water confiscated as you do boarding the Shuttle from Edinburgh to London. I can't move on here without saying something about the chips at Barra Airport- they were awesome! Hand cut, deep fried, wonderful. If you do make it to Barra sometime, do go to the airport for a plate of chips!

It was a fabulous, beautiful sailing across the Sound of Barra to the small island of Eriskay where my journey took me along the west shore, over a causeway and onto South Uist. We met some lovely people on the ferry who happened to live very close to me here in Edinburgh. As it turned out we kept bumping into each other all the way up the islands as often is the case on a touring holiday such as this.

It was another steep climb over Eriskay but before I knew it I was at the causeway taking me onto South Uist where

I had about 10 miles left to do to take me to our pre-booked accommodation in the village of Daliburgh. I say village using the word loosely. Houses and properties don't seem to be arranged in any particular order up here. Thank goodness it was still light when we arrived or we might never have found the place. This was a phenomenon that I would discover is right throughout the Hebrides that there are no streets, no apparent order to anything. How the post man works out where things have to go I have no idea!

We spent the night in Mrs Mcphee's B&B. We went out to find something to eat but neither of us were that hungry so we ended up sitting in the car, in the dark, by a foggy, misty Lochan having a picnic. We dined on breakfast cereal and snacks. When got back and were asked if we had a nice meal, we just said yes thanks, very nice. For some reason we just felt sheepish that we sat in the dark and had cereal! I hoped it was enough of a meal because I knew I had a slightly more demanding cycling ahead of me in the morning. However, I also knew that, staying in a B&B, I'd have a lovely cooked breakfast with the essential Stornaway Black Pudding that I looked forward to very much.

We had a comfortable night in Mrs McPhee's house and really good breakfast to start the day. That was the first time for many years I had stayed in a B&B and it's a strange experience. I found it odd being in someone else's houses with their things around me, and their tastes of décor and soft furnishing. Normally when you go to a hotel everything in non descriptive or neutral, but I felt really strange at first to be in someone's house surrounded by their taste in flowery wallpaper. The black pudding at breakfast made up for everything though and set me up nicely for the day.

It was dry again this morning. Not too cold with a bit of a south west breeze. If it stayed like this all day I thought, it would be a fairly easy day. I needed a bit of boost however. For the first time I was beginning to question why I was doing this in the first place. It was not a particularly nice morning and I was about to get on the bike and cycle 40 miles, for what purpose I asked myself? Then across the car-park I caught sight of a couple of people who we met on the ferry the previous day. It was lovely to see them again and we exchanged a few words and, among other things, they gave me lots of encouragement. I don't think they realised how much benefit they had been to me and it really helped. Just a bit of a chat was enough to help me get underway and, a mile up the road I felt fine again.

This reminded me of the mental health issues I have experienced in my life and how having support from understanding people to talk to and give a bit of encouragement can change everything. I can't believe I am actually mentioning my mental health struggles on my blog for the planet to see. It has taken me a long time to get to this stage where I can feel comfortable about doing that. Who knows, I might write more about this in the future, because believe me, I have no end of material in that department!

The weather was deteriorating, it was clouding over and beginning to rain more persistently. Although the wind was getting up, I remember feeling it but it hadn't yet become a problem. It seemed to be blowing across me and occasionally I got a push from it. I rode on through the rolling hills of South Uist toward Benbecula which, despite the wind, was a pleasant enough cycle. I was really struck by the contrast in the landscape between east and west, the gentle rolling scenery where I was and the mountains towards the east. I passed lots of lochans where I sometimes got a glimpse of a bird of prey, mainly buzzards unfortunately. I'm always hopeful of seeing the majestic Golden Eagle. I generally go by the rule that, if in doubt, it's a buzzard. I had this method confirmed to me whilst on Islay last year when I did see an eagle sitting on a telegraph pole when there was no mistaking, it was huge!

When I crossed from South Uist on to Benbecula I crossed another of the thoughtfully constructed causeways that link many on the smaller islands. With their giant boulders that line the route and the shoreline that drops away from them, I find them really quite beautiful. I had a memory of seeing them featured on the television last year when they became flooded and cars got stuck half way across them in a storm. It wasn't difficult to imagine, it felt very exposed.

At the start of every causeway, there is a triangular road sign that says "CAUTION, Otters Crossing." I got really excited because I would have loved to have seen an otter and I thought my chance had come again. It was the perfect scenario because I am on my bike, they'll never hear me coming, so I could sneak up and get a good look at one. In the distance I saw something move. It was perched on a rock on my right hand side as I looked at the causeway just up ahead. I slowed the bike down and tried to peddle as smoothly and quietly as possible. I saw it move, and could see the shape of its rounded head and muzzle. I was so excited and, as I got near, it turned to look at me and it was then I noticed it was a grey seal. I've never been so disappointed to see a seal before but I was.

I pushed on for the next few miles in the rain over, what felt like, causeway after causeway. I didn't appreciate until I was there just how many tiny islands and how much water there is on the islands. If the light caught the *water in my eyeline the reflections were stunningly beautiful and I felt really lucky to be there. There felt like miles of coastline where the sand just fell away from the sides of the road into an enormous expanse of beautiful beach and space.*

I had arranged to meet my friend Eileen, who was driving the car with all our kit in it for the week, somewhere on Benbecula but I suddenly had a feeling that I had been cycling for a couple of hours now and I hadn't caught sight of her. Normally Eileen would drive a few miles ahead in the car and, when I caught up, we would touch base, and she'd go on ahead again. I realised I hadn't caught sight of her for a couple of hours, it was raining heavily, and I getting cold. I stopped by a modern stone looking building at the side of the road and took myself and the bike into the porch out of the rain. I took out my moby to phone, only to find that there was no phone signal. Suddenly, it felt like a real adventure, I was cold, wet and lost.

By the time I stopped and it had dawned on me that I had probably gone too far and didn't really know where I was, I was soaked to the skin and really starting to get cold. The rain had been coming down quite heavily but I hadn't really realized it, I was just enjoying my cycle.

I came off the road into the car park of what looked like quite a modern building that had been built in slate to perhaps emulate the stonework of long ago. I sheltered in the porch where I noticed the sign on the wall saying Church of Scotland. I thought I had found real refuge but the doors were locked. I took out my mobile telephone to call to see where my support driver had got to only to find I had no signal. In between sheltering in the doorway, I kept running round the outside of the building to try and get a signal. Eventually I got through but wasn't able to tell Eileen where I was before we got cut off again because, in fact, I didn't know where I was.

I think I was there for about 45 minutes, long enough anyway to get very cold and very wet. While I was standing in the doorway taking shelter, I was very conscious that I was being watched by a family in the house opposite who kept peering out the window to see if I was still there. I was trying to make myself look cold by blowing into my hands and wrapping my arms around my shoulders and, in my head, had a fantasy that they might come and place hot coffee in my hands. This was time to meet my good Samaritan. A fantasy it turned out to be however, but as soon as the car arrived I got warmed up with some chocolate and a hot drink.

We spent the night in a B&B just beside the village of Bayhead on North Uist. There was nowhere nearby to eat and the landlady was so kind to us. We bought some delights at the local Co-op and Morag, the owner of the B&B, let us have the run of dining room and sitting room to enjoy our meal and relax. We were both getting tired by this time so having a few hours to chill was great. We had a lovely night's stay there so I feel I have to put a big recommendation here for Morag's B&B, Bayhead, North Uist.

Next morning, I dreaded going out in the rain again but once I got underway and got into a groove, as they say, and the miles soon passed. The weather wasn't good but I still loved the scenery. Along the north coast every so often the road would go quite near the beach and I would get another wonderful view of the stunning beaches there. I crossed yet another causeway, which turned out to be my last, onto Berneray where we got the Ferry to Leverburgh on Harris. Unfortunately I didn't see too much of Berneray other than the ferry terminal where we boarded.

The ferry crossing took about an hour and the rain didn't' seem to be letting up. Our plan was to spend the night in Tarbert about 20 miles from Leverburgh. When we boarded the ferry at Berneray I got myself dried off and warmed up so was dreading going back out in the rain again to push another 20 miles. Fortunately the rain had eased very slightly and lulled me into thinking that it had stopped. I got underway and only a short few miles further on is started to rain again. I was out there now I thought and may as well carry on to make Tarbert that night.

Funnily enough, this particular leg of the journey turned out to be my favourite bit of cycling of the whole week. By the time I got into the Mountains of Harris, there was just a very soft gentle rain, not a breath of wind, and not remotely cold. It just made for a wonderful atmosphere and feeling for going over the hills. I hardly passed another vehicle and felt like I had the island to myself. I had a ball that afternoon despite all my reservations about going back out in the rain. By the time I reached Tarbert I was soaked to the skin but I couldn't have cared less. I was so happy and felt so fulfilled that I was doing it and had such a good time, nothing seemed to matter.

We had difficulty finding accommodation in Tarbert that night. We had gone round several hotels and B&Bs but there seemed to be no room at the Inn. We ordered take away pizza in a local hotel called Hotel Hebrides down at the harbour and, as we were waiting, explained to the manager that we can't find a bed. Her name was Emily and could not have been more helpful. Emily let us sit in the bar and eat out take away pizza there, while she phoned around to try and find us a bed. AS time went on we became more and more worried that we would have ot sleep in the car. We had sleeping bags with us so it was an option but we were trying our best to avoids having to do that. As it it got later we really thought we might have to do that. Fortunately at 9.30 pm, we found a guest house with space for us. We were so grateful to Emily and the effort she put in to find us a bed for the night. We have a very comfortable night at Flora's Guest house and all was well.

Cycling over Harris from Tarbert to Callanish was just wonderful, the weather was fine, the road was quiet and with a cross-tail wind most of the way cycling was not too difficult. Although the mountains of Harris were truly spectacular they, without doubt, presented the biggest physical challenge. Shortly after leaving Tarbert and passing through a few villages a beautiful bay called Ceann an Ora stretches out in an expanse of space on the left hand side. I saw a road on the other side of the bay which I thought might be the one I had to take. It meandered along the side of the hill and gradually gained height into the mountains. However this turned out not to be the route although before long I was wishing it had been.

The road then took me east onto what turned out to be the most difficult part of the whole journey. The mountain of Tarsaval is the highest part of the whole journey and the road wound steeply up the side. It was the steepest or biggest mountain pass I have cycled so far. It was difficult and while I was plodding my way up, I was wondering if I really wanted to make a habit of this kind of cycling. I have lots of routes in Scotland I would like to do in the future and it was as if this was giving me a little taste of what it would be like doing some serious mountains in the Highlands.

Being on top of the mountains there made up for the climb several times over. The view was spectacular and the feeling was lovely. I felt like I was getting near and was in sight of completing my challenge and that felt good. I just had to finish today and that would give me

40 miles to complete the following morning to reach Ness. I enjoyed cycling the rest of that road and was having so much fun that I missed the sign to say that I was on Lewis, the last island on my journey. It was after I had stopped and met Eileen that she told me I had reached Lewis. I just had 7 miles left to do to the west of the island to Callanish where we would stop for the night.

This 7 miles turned out to be the most difficult part of the whole trip. The road went west over open moorland directly into a very strong wind and, with little shelter I was up against it all the way. Unfortunately I had to stop and eat only a couple of miles from my destination because I had the feeling of running on empty. This is one lesson I have learned the hard way which is to know when you are running low and to stop and refuel before you suffer the 'knock' as we call it in cycling terms.

That evening we stayed in the village of Callanish and visited the famous stone circle. What made it more special was that it was the day of the full moon. We had our evening meal at the stones and took so many photographs. I found it just amazing to think that these stones have been there a minimum of 4000, but possibly as much as 6000 years, and still the purpose of them is unknown. It is a very special experience going there and a must for anybody visiting Lewis and the Outer Hebrides.

On the whole, the trip went really smoothly. My driver was never very far away with the car, I had no mechanical trouble with the bike and the weather was mixed. The important thing was that I had checked out the direction of the prevailing wind being south to north so the wind was predominantly on my back. We only lost each other the once.

The most challenging bit of the trip was cycling over Harris but strangely it was the bit of the journey I enjoyed the most. It rained a good bit in the middle of the week and I do remember being on the ferry from North Uist to Leverburgh on Harris and not being able to get enough food inside me to satisfy my hunger. I would have eaten anything I could get my hands on. I was so Hungry. We had to sit inside the cabin during the crossing because the rain was persistent or 'dinging on' as we say. As we got nearer to Leverburgh my spirits became heavier and heavier because our next stop was Tarbert. I had another 20 miles to push up and over bumpy terrain and there was no sign of the weather easing. We were just outside the ferry port where we got the bike out of the car. I got on all my waterproofs and filled my pockets with all the munch bars I thought I would need. Before long I was underway again and Leverburgh was behind me. The first stage felt difficult but I soon settled into my rhythm and the miles started to pass.

The rain didn't stop that entire afternoon but this would turn out to be the section of the entire trip that I enjoyed the most. I would do this again, in the rain, in a heartbeat. Harris is beautiful with its long sandy beaches in ever changing colours that would take a better wordsmith than me to describe to you. The rugged mountains and silky-smooth roads just make it a joy to cycle. Although the lessons I learned that afternoon stuck with me for a while. Firstly, I realised that the biggest battle or barrier to anything is not the distance we have to travel, but the distance between our ears. Our mind and how we manage it is key to everything. There were mornings throughout the trip, just like that afternoon, when I thought I can't ride today. I thought I needed to rest, I felt bad, or lethargic. A few miles up the road however, I felt fantastic again and was loving being on my bike. There are so many thoughts that stop us taking the first steps to achieve our goals and live out our dreams. However, they are just thoughts and have to be seen for what they are. More often than not, they are irrational, false, and without any evidence at all. If we can manage our minds and quell the irrational doubts that we have, how much more could we achieve?

We learn things about ourselves and our lives often in the most unlikely circumstances. I set out on this trip because I was fortunate enough to have the support of my good friend Eileen to be able to do it, and I wanted to get my new career, or whatever it turned out to be, underway with a big adventure. By doing this trip however, I learned another lesson that I wasn't really expecting. At that time in my life I was doing a lot of serious cycling. I used to train, go spin classes and I was chasing after a road club. I use the term "chasing after" because that's the best way to describe it. I had been cycling with them for a number of years by this time and spent all my time making myself unhappy by trying, and not managing, to keep up. The reality was that I was cycling with fit and able-bodied people and there was no way I was ever going to keep up. I was trying to measure my ability against theirs which was completely unrealistic. I have cerebral palsy and it was unrealistic to measure my progress or performance against, not just able-bodied but really athletic and fit able-bodied people.

The only person I measure my ability or performance against is my own. I'm done comparing myself to others. This really hit home for me at the end of the Hebridean Way. I was just desperate to get the lighthouse at the Butt of Lewis, take photographs and text them to say 'look I've done it, I achieved this thing.' That's exactly what I did only to meet with the realisation that these people couldn't have cared a toot for what I had achieved. The best they could do was make light of it by making a joke. "Time to take the bike out of the car for a photograph David," was one of their responses. Whatever I did I was never going to meet their standards of approval and, I ask myself now, why would I want to anyway. The only person I ever need to satisfy is myself. I realised then that I had done that expedition partly to get my new career, or whatever, underway but that wasn't the whole story. A big part of my motivation was to 'prove' something to other people, seeking their approval or wanting to be in their gang. These were all the wrong reasons to do anything. From that time onwards I realised that the only person I need to, or want to, prove anything to is myself. I felt like a hard lesson at the time, people I thought were friends and on my side turned out to be not. I learned from it and grew from it. Now I enjoy my cycling and indeed all my sports are more than I ever have. Whatever I do, I do only to make myself happy. It's incredibly liberating the moment you realise that you only have to satisfy yourself and the incredible range of things available to you that enable you to do that.

This isn't the only cycling adventure that I've completed up until now. In September 2018 I, supported by a charity, cycled one of the longest routes and most demanding routes I have cycled so far. The Caledonia Way stenches from Campbeltown in Kintyre and runs right through the Great Glen up to Inverness. I cycled the 240 mile route in 7 days and what a wonderful adventure it was. On tiny back roads most of the way and along canal towpaths the route takes in some of the most spectacular scenery in Scotland. I did this with a lovely bunch of people and it was a really positive experience. Cycling is something I feel about doing at my one level and being able to do routes like this is a real joy and I hope to do more in the future.

Chapter 9

After I started my Blog, writing about my experiences in Outdoor Sports, I was hungry for more. I had finally found what I enjoyed the most and just wanted to fill my life with Adventures. So I looked around for more opportunities. Many years had passed since I had been hillwalking as I did most of my walking when I had been at the University In Dundee. I had climbed around 25 Munros (mountains over 900M) in those days. Interestingly I had kept a detailed record all this time of the mountains I had climbed. I must have thought I would go back to it one day, and that's exactly what happened. Having found my passion again for outdoor sport, I began to wonder if I might carry on climbing the Scottish Mountains where I left off all these years ago.

I scoured the internet and started searching for walking groups or organisations. I came across a group called 'Walk Highland ' who meet up regularly for walks. 'Walk Highland' is a great website with excellent information about all sorts of walks in Scotland, big and small. A community of people have evolved from that website who meet four times a year in a hostel for a weekend in the mountains. There was to be a meet up in Glencoe so "in for a penny, in for a pound" I thought, I put my name down to go.

I was naturally apprehensive when I drove north to join a group of people where I knew nobody. Would I feel accepted or be like a spanner in the works being the only disabled person there? I'd have been surprised if other disabled people had turned up at any of their meets and

said they wanted to go up the mountain, but that's exactly what I did. I remember at the time trying to get myself to look at it as a social experiment as well as anything else! I was made welcome and met some really nice people.

During the first evening people were discussing what routes they wanted to walk the following day and what mountains they wanted to tackle. We were in Kinlochleven on the edge of the 'Grey Corries' and most people were heading up that way. The ' Ring of Steall ' was a big walk with many peaks and I knew that I certainly wasn't going to be attempting that any time soon. I didn't know what to do. It had been so many years since I had been up the mountains and I didn't know what my capabilities would be. Thankfully after dinner I got chatting to someone called Malcolm. I explained the situation and why I was there and he agreed to go out walking with me the following day. We agreed to do a relatively smaller mountain in Glencoe. I say relatively because all the mountains are big up there. I had climbed in Glencoe before and I had completed two of the peaks there so I thought I'd be fine. We decided to try 'Buachaille Etive Beag.'

The ascent went fine and I was really enjoying it. It felt great to be back out on the mountains. It was a clear day and the views were great and everything was going well. Eventually I turned to start coming back down and shortly afterwards pain started to creep in. My hip joints and lower back got worse and worse and by the time I was only halfway back down the mountain I was in chronic pain. I still had a long way to go to get back to the car. There were lots of other people on the mountain by that time it must have been obvious that I was in pain. People were stopping to ask if I was ok and even offering to carry my pack. By the time I got back to the car I was in phenomenal amounts of pain. It was such a shame because it took the shine off a great experience. Just like every other experience I really learned something from it. I learned about having grit and determination but, at the same time, knowing your limitations!

Below is an extract from my blog describing the whole experience:

THE CHALLENGE OF THE MOUNTAINS AND FINDING COMMUNITY IN KINLOCHLEVEN

Inspiration

The inspiration to climb the Scottish Mountains I believe, once inside you, is a feeling that never leaves you. Twenty years have passed since I last climbed a Munro. Recently my motivation, inspiration and passion for hillwalking flooded into my system again and last weekend I had the chance to rediscover what I have missed. Since I started writing my outdoor sports blog last year I have embraced fully an outdoor life. I wanted to see if I still had what it takes to climb the mountains and meet similarly minded people to do it with along the way.

The Weekend.

A few months ago I came across the website of 'Walk Highlands.' This is a tremendous online resource for anybody considering, walking in Scotland. There is a lot of information about walks in the Munros and at lower levels too. Basically there is something for everyone no matter what level you are walking at. As well as providing information, there is a forum enabling walkers to communicate, share walk reports and make arrangements for meets. I was on the website recently looking for opportunities to rekindle my walking experience. There was a weekend meet in Kinlochleven. I booked myself a bed in the hostel for two nights and decided to go and see what would happen.

Arrival

Not knowing who else would turn up at the meet, I was a little apprehensive when I arrived on the Friday evening. I've not seen other people with cerebral palsy out on the mountains and I suspected neither had they! Had a disabled person ever pitched up at one of these meets before? Very soon, I felt very welcome indeed and found myself in conversation and laughs with many. It was a lovely atmosphere and I had a good feeling about the weekend ahead.

With such a passage of time since I last climbed a Munro, I had no idea if I would be able to do this. As the evening wore on people were discussing plans for the walk. I knew I could join any of the walks but I didn't want to take on more than I could do and end up holding people back. Before I travelled to Kinlochleven I had decided on the walk that I wanted to do. I wanted to tackle the majestic Buachialle Etive Beag *in Glencoe. I have climbed its sister, the Buachialle Etive Mor over 20 years ago and just loved walking in that area. Thankfully I found someone happy to tackle it with me and so I was looking forward to the walk very much.*

The Walk

Conditions could hardly have been better when we set off. It was a beautiful morning. We followed the very well trodden path that leaves the car-park closest to the waterfall in Glencoe. After about a kilometre, the path splits where one goes into Glen Etive, the other up towards the saddle of the mountain. This part of the walk went more or less straight up, what felt like, a giant staircase. So much effort had gone into constructing a path with very large boulders. We soon gained height and gazed at some great views over to the Aonach Eagach ridge. The path continued upwards fairly relentlessly until it levelled out somewhat as we approached the saddle of the mountain. At this point I decided just to enjoy the views and not climb any further. I was Glad I did!

The Descent

I felt fine when I started heading back down but I was beginning to feel tremendous strain on my thighs and hip joints. Taking my time I kept a steady pace and used my walking poles to steady myself. Not much further down however, I could feel my legs starting to grow painfully sore. I was ready for my lunch but didn't want to stop because I knew, if I did, my legs would seize up. Determined to make it down over the most difficult part of the descent before I stopped, I kept on. I was in a lot of pain by now but I carried on. Some people who were on their way up who asked me if I was alright because I was obviously looking quite wobbly by that stage. Eventually I got back down as far I wanted to before I stopped for something to eat. My legs and lower back were in agony but fortunately we only had a kilometre or so to go back to the car. The last kilometre was extremely challenging and I had to keep stopping due to the severe pain in my joints. I was so grateful to see the car again.

Reflection

All my apprehensions about going on this 'Mountain Meet' quickly evaporated and I experienced a great weekend. I met some lovely people, felt very welcome and I had a lot of fun. I had wanted to try something like this for a while and didn't know how I would get on. Sometimes when you have any form of disability, it can take an extra bit of courage to turn up. This can be particularly so when the emphasis is on a physical activity. All my fears were needless and I had a great time.

The walking experience itself however, has left me feeling very frustrated indeed. I can't put into words how much energy and determination doing something like this sucks out of me. As well as being in a lot of severe pain at the time, it really wiped me out for a few days afterwards. I do, of course, ask myself if it's worthwhile and sometimes the answer eludes me. I don't want to experience that level of pain and exhaustion on the hill again. However, I am still determined to enjoy the mountains and make them part of my life. I am very keen to climb Munros again one day and I intend to try and build my strength up to enable me to do that. I am also realistic and I will look for other ways to enjoy the wonderful mountains. Either way, I hope to attend the next 'Walk Highlands' and have as much fun as I had this weekend.

My experience of Glencoe that day was a great learning experience but wouldn't put me off wanting to be in the mountains however. If anything it reinforced that this is where my passions lie and made me more determined to follow my heart's desire. It did make me want to explore other ways of being and experiencing the outdoors. I suspect for a long time I thought that in order to enjoy the outdoors, or to live the outdoor life, you had to be out and achieving. I suspect many people think the same. That you have to get out and climb mountains, kayak the rivers or be a fell runner is not true. Discovering this made me determined to find my own ways to be in the outdoors. Nowadays I'm happy to be in my tent with a nice view, cooking a nice meal. Or having a gentle bike ride on a forest track. Being in the outdoors to me now is not about achievement, but just about being. Of course, if you do want to set yourself tasks that's fine, but if you just want to be, then that's also fine too. I think there is a lesson for life here. Many of us are constantly striving to achieve the next thing, to get a better job, to jump up the ladder or to make that extra bit of money. In doing this we forget to enjoy the moments and enjoy what we have right here and now. One thing I have learned over the years is to try not to compare myself to others or, if I do, try to compare myself to people throughout the world and not just in my backyard.

Just being in the wilderness or a remote place soon became enough for me and this was something that would be reinforced to me on my first visit to Knoydart. Sometimes, when you go to visit a place, it gets into your system or under your skin and that's precisely what happened to me on my first visit to Knoydart. This isolated peninsula off the west coast of Scotland is most easily reached by boat. The nearest road is nine miles away. When you sail up Loch Nevis and the tiny village of Inverie comes into view, you really feel like you are off the beaten track. Knoydart is a huge piece of land with a very small population of people living there. Described by many as the "Last True Wilderness" its tiny population owns and manages the land. For many people including me it is a really lovely place. I love the remoteness and isolation there, the fact that nature is bigger than anything else. It is very healing and I feel most at peace up there. In the past I probably would have wanted to climb all the mountains on the peninsula and I have to admit I've had a go at one of them. Now, however, just being there is enough for me. I'm happy to sit by the shore for a morning or ride my bike along the valley. The mountains there are too much for me, I know that. But my appreciation of nature and my joy of just being there, is greater than it ever was.

Knoydart is now somewhere I try to visit every year, it's like just something I need. I really fell in love with Knoydart the very first time I visited and I hope it remains a part of life for many years to come. After my first visit, I wanted to try to capture my experience in Blog form.

Below is the post I published which I hope will give you a flavour of it.

DISCOVERING KNOYDART: SCOTLAND'S LAST TRUE WILDERNESS

Knoydart is a very special place. A peninsula on the west coast of Scotland accessed only by boat, it has all the feelings of a remote Scottish island. Staying in the village of Inverie, I went there recently to explore Scotland's last true wilderness.

Standing on the pier at Mallaig, I couldn't believe how many bags we had. The pier was strewn with luggage, not just ours of course, but several families worth of bags. Everyone taking enough to survive the week. There are no grocery stores as such on Knoydart so it is essential to take provisions with you. There are, however, a couple of places you can pick up basic supplies. The post office sells a few household goods and provisions. The Knoydart Foundation has its own shop in the village and it has a freezer full of excellent venison and a small Off Licence for important stocks of booze.

You really get the feeling you are going somewhere off the beaten track particularly when you scan your eyes round the harbour. The boat to Knoydart doesn't leave from the larger ferry terminal for the Caledonian McBrayne services sailing to the Hebrides. Surrounded by fishing boats a small vessel with a cabin big enough for a dozen or so people appears round the corner and docks discretely alongside the harbour steps. Men throw ropes to tie up, while others help passengers step over the side of the vessel and up the steps onto the shore on their return to Mallaig from Inverie.

We get the signal to board and before long a human chain had formed the length of the harbour steps. Bags of all shapes and sizes were passed from one pair of hands to another. There was something really lovely about how naturally a human chain formed between *strangers and everybody helped out to put all the luggage on board. Bags, canoes and even a didgeridoo passed through peoples' hands as the boat slowly loaded up. Once on the boat, the goods were covered with a thick tarpaulin to prevent them becoming wet from any spray that might come over the bow during the short forty minute crossing. The boat sailed to the right from the harbour and conversations began between people from several nationalities speaking in different languages.*

The sail up Loch Nevis and into Inverie felt just magical. Surrounded by the most beautiful of Scottish Highland scenery, the whitewashed cottages that line the front of the village came closer into view. How lucky I felt, that this picturesque location was going to be my home for the next week. I couldn't wait to explore the forests and rugged coastline that stretched into the distance. Bags were unloaded into the back of Landrovers that arrived onto the pier to meet the boat. After being a hive of activity, the pier was soon empty and deserted again as visitors were taken to their accommodation.

We were staying in a traditional style cottage called Tigh Na Feidh, in the village of Inverie. This had once been a crofter's cottage and boasted magnificent views over Loch Nevis and to the hills beyond. It was very comfortably furnished inside in a very charming traditional manner. It wasn't long before we settled in and looked forward to evening drinks in the sitting room around the wood burning fire.

Knoydart is a wonderful place to enjoy the outdoors. Whether its canoeing, mountain biking, walking or fishing, this is wonderful environment to be in. Many people go to Knoydart for its wilderness experience and enjoy the isolation in some spectacular scenery. We spent the first morning walking to explore the village and its immediate surroundings. Some beautiful woodlands line the road that takes you along towards the Kilchoan Estate.

I had forgotten how much I enjoyed sea fishing and I was thrilled to have the opportunity to fish again. When I was child I loved fishing with my father from his small boat. We would launch it off Dunbar on the East Lothian coast and often come back with lots of fish.

Unfortunately, fishing is one of the few things I can't do on my own due to the dexterity required to tie lines. So, I took advantage of having some help this week and spent a few evenings fishing off the pier. The mackerel I caught made a tasty supper one evening.

One of the things I most wanted to do was to climb

Ladhar Bienne, the highest Munro on the peninsula. We planned to hire a Landrover to take us into the valley to the foot of the mountain so as to shorten the route. Unfortunately, I have been finding walking very difficult at the moment so climbing a Munro was not an option for me. People who follow my blog will have seen a recent post about the difficulties I am experiencing in walking. However, I discovered a new interest which I never knew could be so much fun, and that was driving the dirt tracks with a Landrover.

Of course, not having many roads suitable for a vehicle on Knoydart, there isn't very far you can go. In an easterly direction from Inverie there are two roads, one is off road and the other is tarmac. One of them leads to a small cove called Airor. What a wonderful journey it was past the headland with some magnificent views over to the islands of Rhum and Skye. At the end of the road was the most remote of little cafes with a lovely selection of food and beautiful home baking. Situated in a lovely bay it had fantastic views over the beach and across to Skye.

The other extremely 'off-road' road from Inverie leads six miles to a farm at a place called Inverguseran. A really beautiful journey through the wilderness takes you into the valley where walkers might begin the ascent of

Ladhar Bienne. This was truly beautiful and felt very wild indeed. To add to the atmosphere we came across a stalker who was saddling up two ponies to go up and take the deer off the hill. For as long as I can remember I have wanted to go stalking, I find it a nice thing to do. I'm hoping to get the opportunity to do this someday. Although climbing the Munro wasn't possible for me this time, the experience of being there was really wonderful.

I've visited many parts of Scotland over recent years and had some amazing experiences. I have to say however that Knoydart is a very special place and already I am longing to go back there. The isolation, the peace, and the feeling of true wilderness make it just magical There are no ferries arriving each day bringing hundreds of tourists. The majority of people there are those who live there. Although this is part of the Scottish mainland, it really feels like island life. Just things like the old cars, and the lack of road signs make it feel very isolated. There is a lovely farm shop on the Kilchoan Estate selling some nice things that has an honesty box for people to leave their money. Doors are seldom locked and keys are left in cars giving a beautiful feel of community and trust.

There are those who would like ferry companies such as Caledonian Macbrayne to begin running a scheduled *service to the peninsula. This would indeed bring many people and money into the community. There would however be a price to pay for this. More infrastructure would be required to support a greater number of visitors and this would change the feel of the place. Before long Knoydart would require more amenities, shops and cafes. One can't help feeling that something special would then be lost forever. I hope Knoydart remains a true wilderness and the already fragile community there survives for many generations to come.*

Campaigning For Change

In the same way as years previously I had found a cause that I was passionate about and where I wanted to instigate change. I started writing years ago as a direct result of unemployment and the apparent discrimination that disabled people faced in the employment forum. Now I was writing about something that made me happy and that I felt really passionate about. I thought about the struggles I had faced at times as a disabled person in trying to achieve the same opportunities as other people to experience and enjoy the outdoors. I wanted to start raising awareness in order to make it easier for other disabled people to travel and access places which might have been off limits to them. So that's exactly what I did.

The John Muir Trust makes an award every year to someone to do something worthwhile that will both increase knowledge and raise awareness of the great outdoors. The ' Des Rubens and Bill Wallace Grant,' is given to an individual every year to enable them to go and do something in the outdoors that they otherwise wouldn't be able to. I was lucky enough to be the recipient of the award in 2017. My focus was to work on observing access for disabled people. I had always wanted to visit the Orkney Islands knowing how steeped in archaeological history they were. Sadly ancient sites are not always accessible to those with mobility difficulties. I proposed to go to Orkney and report on just how accessible some of these places were. What I found was really mixed and I realised how difficult it can be for disabled people to see things in the outdoors that most able-bodied people take for granted. By undertaking this project, it really inspired me to look more closely at disability access to the great outdoors. Many people think that being able to spend time outdoors, or spend time in the countryside is a right, as something anybody can do. Although if you are disabled or mobility impaired, it is not as easy as people think. I really try to raise awareness and help to create opportunities for disabled people to do just that.

Below are two extracts from my blog that I thought would help highlight the type of work I set out to do.

LOOKING AHEAD TO THE PAST

The John Muir Trust is a conservation charity dedicated to protecting and enhancing wild places. Each year the John Muir Trust award a small number of grants to individuals, to enable them to visit and explore wild places. Grants are to enable people to go and experience wild environments while, at the same time, raise awareness for the protection of wild places. I am thrilled to say that I have been awarded one of the grants this year. Later this month I will embark on a tour of Orkney to report on disability access to the fascinating archaeological sites.

Earlier in the year, I had the idea that I wanted to visit Orkney. Readers of my blog will know that last year I cycled the length of the Outer Hebrides and, among other things, visited Callanish. The 5,000 year old neolithic stone circle was a truly amazing site and it really ingnited my enthusiasm for taking a look into the past. I had heard from many people that Orkney was an amazing place and just steeped in archaeological history.

Before long I was looking at organised tours of Orkney that I could join. As well as being phenomenally expensive, one of the tours specifically said that it was not suitable for disabled people. This, like a red rag to a bull, made me even more determined to see for myself. With the grant from the John Muir Trust, I would be visiting Orkney later this month to visit the archaeological sites for myself. I am very excited about this. As part of my ongoing work, I will be reporting on the accessibility of the sites for disabled people and way in which disabled people can also have a glimpse into the past as well. I hope that by doing this I will help improve access to tourism for disabled people to allow them to enjoy wild places as much as everyone else can.

ACCESSING THE PAST ON ORKNEY

I have been lucky enough to visit Orkney lately and I

had a really interesting time. My trip was to carry out detailed research. Funded by the 'John Muir Trust Des Rubens and Bill Wallace Grant,' I went to Orkney to investigate disability access across the archaeological sites. The idea for this investigation came after the discovery that some tour operators specifically say their tours are not suitable for disabled people. I wanted to discover for myself and, thanks to the John Muir Trust, Des Rubens and Bill Wallace Grant, that is exactly what I did.

Accessing the Past

Orkney is a wonderful place rich in archaeological sites. There have been many television documentaries and books written about them. Most people who know anything about Orkney have heard of Maes Howe, Scara Brae and the Ring of Brodgar. Although these sites are very well known, there are many more sites both on mainland Orkney and the surrounding islands.

Site Management

Historic Scotland are a national agency whose remit is to protect the ancient relics and natural environment of Scotland. Members, like myself, obtain unlimited access to all the ancient sites of castles and monuments. Membership money allows Historic Scotland to protect the sites. They also make the places accessible by providing visitors centres and laying on events.

Being able to access and see for yourself the sites of ancient civilisations is really important for all of us. I feel that it changes outlooks on our lives and what we value about our society. However, these prestigious locations are a lot more difficult for disabled people to see. The preservation is very important, but can we strike a balance between preservation and access for all.

The sites are managed by Historic Scotland and I wanted to see for myself just how disabled people might access them.

On the Ground

Over the course of the week I visited as many of the archaeological sites as possible. It was a truly amazing experience. Below I have given a short description of a few of the sites and commented on the accessibility.

Accessibility

While discussing access to the archaeological sites, it is important first to recognise the importance of *maintaining and preserving the integrity of the site. These sites date back 5000 years and really ought to be left exactly how they were found. Many of the sites therefore could not be made accessible without damaging them. Maes Howe for example, as well as the other burial tombs, could not be made accessible. One has crawl into them with a torch and even the most able of us might find this difficult.*

Possible Changes

Although it is important to maintain the archaeological sites exactly as they are, this may be an excuse for Historic Scotland to overlook disability. There is an excellent visitor centre at Scara Brae that is fully accessible, and a good path around most of the site. Apart from this, one can't help feeling that disability has been overlooked.

There are numerous sites that could easily be made more accessible for small amounts of money. For example, it would be so easy to create some walkways that would enable a wheelchair user to see The Ring of Brodgar, Stones of Stenness or the Broch of Gurness. Gates could be made much wider and ramps could be built at places such as Birsay. All these changes would not in any way destroy the integrity of the site and make them much easier for people to see. This would benefit both disabled people and non disabled. Where sites are completely inaccessible perhaps modern technology could be utilised more to create a better visitor experience for less able people.

I think Historic Scotland need to take a look at all of their key sites and ask themselves what could be done to make them more accessible for all. One fails to see why this has been so badly neglected. It is so important for everyone, able-bodied or not, to be able to have a window into the past. I hope groups might start to put gentle pressure onto Historic Scotland to encourage them to consider increasing accessibility to other important places and not just Skara Brae.

Accessing the Mountains

Thinking about the difficulties I've had at times in my life to obtain access to the outdoors, particularly onto the mountains, made me wonder how other disabled people might do that too. I am fortunate that I can do small walks, but I can't do anything like the walking that I used to be able to do. For some reason as I've got older

I find walking more and more difficult. Although I still love the mountains, the views and emotions when you are at the top is like no other feeling. In September, 2017 I visited Cairngorm Mountain and made use of the funicular railway. I went up on the Funicular then booked onto a guided walk that took me right to the top of Caringorm. The view was amazing and I loved being up there and looking out across the Cairngorm Plateau. This is a fantastic resource that helps people of any ability to get a true mountain experience. The funicular railway was such a controversial project at the time it was developed. It was vehemently opposed by many who thought it was a disaster for the environment. Personally I appreciated the way it enabled people of any ability access to wild places which otherwise they would never reach. It's used in the winter by disabled skiers to help them up the mountain too. Sadly, as I write these pages, the funicular railway is out of operation and has been for the last twelve months. Engineers discovered a structural fault and deemed it unsafe for use. The bill to repair it will run into millions of pounds and the debate right now is who is going to pick up the tab. I hope however that by the time you are reading this that it is all up and running again and helping people to access the mountain who otherwise wouldn't be able to experience its joys.

Below is an extract from my blog that I wrote after my visit to the top of Cairngorm. I really loved the experience and hope I can do it again sometime.

EXPERIENCING THE WONDERS OF CAIRNGORM USING THE FUNICULAR RAILWAY.

Cairngorm Mountain is home to Scotland's only Funicular Railway. Opened in 2001 the line takes thousands of visitors up and down Cairngorm Mountain to the highest cafe in the UK, the Ptarmigan Restaurant, which sits at over 3,500ft about sea level. Cairngorm is a hive of activity at all times of year with thousands of skiers in the wintertime, and many visitors over the summer months experiencing the wonders of the mountain.

The funicular railway was, from its very inception, shrouded in controversy and to this day still somewhat divides opinion. From the moment it was first proposed it was vehemently opposed by sections of the environmental lobby on the grounds of its lasting impact on a very special and already very fragile site of scientific interest. First proposed as far back as the 1950's, and then spoken of again in the 60s, only in 2001 did this project reach its completion because of all the challenges. When the railway finally opened in December 2001, many thought of it as the greatest Christmas present the Highlands had ever seen. Jobs on the mountain, and the increase in visitor numbers would bring long needed prosperity and investment for the tourist industry in the surrounding area. Others however mourned for what they saw as an environmental disaster.

Cairngorm itself is one of the biggest mountains in the UK. At over 4000 feet it is the sixth highest mountain in the United Kingdom and gives its name to the whole range of mountains. The name Cairngorm translates as 'Blue Mountain' and from a distance it is easy to appreciate why it got this name. Ironically however, anyone walking on the mountain will notice the geology of a very red type of stone so historically Cairngorm was known as the 'Red Mountain'. Red or Blue, this mountain is very special for many different reasons and hundreds of thousands of people flock to experience its riches every year.

Being one of the highest peaks, and giving its name to the range, it is on many walkers 'to do' list. Mountaineers scale it at all times of the year either walking or climbing. I had wanted to experience the summit of Cairngorm for a long time so I took the opportunity and made use of the funicular railway to reach the top. One of my motivations was to see and experience the spectacular Cairngorm Plateau. I wanted to see for myself this great expanse of mountain which joins several peaks including Cairngorm and Ben Macdui. Infamous for its exposure, it attracts thousands of mountaineers each year in all weathers. Sadly, many have lost their lives there as a result of the changing weather and exposure to the elements.

We booked onto a guided walk which is the only way to the summit of Cairngorm while using the funicular railway. In order to satisfy the environmentalists, one of the conditions of building the railway was to minimise the impact of visitors. One of the ways this is achieved is by containing people and not letting them wander onto the mountain unless with a guide. Of course, if you walk up the mountain from ground level you are free to wander but, using the funicular railway you must book onto a tour. This makes sense to me, given how many people venture into the mountains without the necessary equipment or experience. Many lives could be put at risk by allowing ill clad, tourists in sand shoes to wander out onto the mountain. I was delighted to reach the Ptarmigan stop and have the opportunity to reach the top with the Ranger.

It's a relatively short walk up to the summit from the Ptarmigan restaurant with only about 500 metres of ascent. The well-constructed paths are sectioned off, again to contain people and minimise environmental damage. We were very lucky to be joined by our guide Gerry, who gave us a real insight into the geology and history of the mountain.

I was hoping to see, or at least hear a Ptarmigan. Very shy but very beautiful birds they spend most of the time on the ground and only fly if they have to. A grey-brown colour in the summer they, like the mountain hare, change their coat in the winter and go all white. This gives them protection from predators from above. We did however see some beautiful reindeer. Although these are wild animals, they were very tame indeed and allowed us to get very close to them. They live up there all year round and are a native species to Norway.

As we approached the summit, views were just spectacular as weather conditions were near perfect. Looking over Cairngorm Plateau was just amazing. This vast wilderness is inspiring. We could see many mountains in all directions and it was good to name many of them. It was a fantastic experience and it has left me with an enthusiasm for more.

I got the feeling that the funicular railway, far from being an environmental disaster, is a wonderful resource for many different reasons. As well as the enormous economic prosperity it brings to the area, it enables people of all abilities to experience the mountains. I don't think mountains should be sacred places reserved only for the fit and able. The experience of being up a mountain is so motivating and inspiring I don't think it's fair to deny the experience to anyone who seeks it. Being able to use the funicular like this so that anybody can experience the pleasure of being up a mountain is a truly great thing. I felt very much at peace with the impact on the environment. It is very contained and only really impacts on one side of a mountain in a vast area.

The ski area was there long before the train. Ski areas in the summertime never look pretty. The mountain organisation 'Natural Retreats 'do a fantastic job managing and containing its impact as well as keeping people safe.

I hope to return to Cairngorm and use the railway again in the near future. I would like to go further afield and even camp out on the Cairngorm Plateau. This would be a truly wonderful experience and one that I would treasure. I feel really hungry to experience the mountains. Unfortunately my walking ability has not enabled me to venture far recently without substantial amounts of pain, or indeed more than I'm prepared to tolerate. I will be looking into ways of making this dream possible soon and hope that I can report back on what a wonderful experience it is.

When I started talking about or raising awareness of access to the outdoors, suddenly people seamed really interested in what I was doing. Before long I was being asked to write articles for magazines. This is an example of one of the first pieces I wrote for and outdoor publication.

DISABLED PEOPLE DESERVE BETTER ACCESS TO THE OUTDOORS

Having access to the outdoors is sometimes taken for granted. However, for disabled people finding opportunities to spend time in the wilderness can be more difficult. I was lucky enough to write this article for Mountaineering Scotland Magazine and share a bit of my experience.

The outdoors have always been a part of my life. Growing up in rural East Lothian, I spent much of my childhood walking hills and beaches with my family. Having Cerebral Palsy of course could make things more challenging for me. My stamina and ability was not as good as it is now. However, I never saw this as something that might stop me but rather just made me more determined.

As I moved through my teenage years and into adulthood, my passion for the outdoors continued to grow. In my early twenties I discovered the Munros and during my time at University with the Hillwalking Society I managed to head out and begin Munro bagging. I would go out at weekends either with the club or with friends made through the club. It became clear quite early on that, much as I loved walking, I didn't have the same energy and stamina as most of my contemporaries. When we climbed the mountains, I would invariably have to descend earlier and walks would take me much longer than the average person. I didn't seem to matter to the University Society and I made friends with understanding, compassionate people who would accompany me hill walking.

My walking ability was never really a problem until well after I left university and settled again in Edinburgh. It was at that time I would approach mainstream clubs and try to find people to go walking with. It was then that I ran into difficulties and one that would continue throughout my adult life. Finding people and opportunities to go walking has been difficult and, so much so, I gave up mountaineering for many years. I got so frustrated at people's lack of patience and lack of support from clubs that I really didn't think I could put myself in that position any longer. I had resigned myself to the fact that the Mountains were not going to be part of my life. Before I knew it 20 years had drifted by but, unbeknown to me, I still had a spark inside me for the mountains.

I have rediscovered my passion for the mountains in recent times and I'm still hopeful of finding more open minded people to walk with. I was aware though that I could well come up against a similar range of problems that I had experienced all those years ago. Many of us live in quite pressurised times and individual leisure time is very precious. People want, and quite rightly so, to get the most out of the spare time that they do have, so spending a day walking at a slower pace is not very appealing. Disabled participation in outdoor sports is still relatively low, and that might be for reasons such as,

- *Mountaineering is dangerous and involves a certain amount of risk.*

- *People generally don't like the idea of being, or feeling like they are, 'responsible' for another person on the hills.*

- *Peoples' leisure time is often short and they want to achieve as much as possible in it.*

- *People always think someone else will have the time but not them.*

I think there is another aspect of people walking with disabled people just once, as if they have 'done their bit' but they would not make a regular commitment. There are still a lot of attitudinal barriers that prevent disabled people taking part in outdoor sport. For example

- *Many people don't imagine outdoor sport is an*

option for disabled people

* *Others tend to make decisions of behalf of disabled people*

* *Disabled people are not seen as equal outdoor partners*

There can be no doubt that sporting opportunities for disabled people are improving and this is, in part, due to the success of the Paralympic movement and London 2012. There is, however, still a long way to go in terms of outdoor sport and mountaineering. It is here that clubs have an important role to play. Thankfully many clubs now have an equality or inclusion policy which covers all minority groups and not just disability. These policies try to insure that nobody is treated differently on the grounds of gender, race, disability or sexual orientation. In the case of disability however, and if there is some kind of physical impairment involved, such as in the case of disability, it is more complicated than just a change in attitude.

To include a disabled person in a mountaineering or walking club, it takes more organisation and planning. On club activity weekends for example, there could be volunteers who agree to walk at a slower pace to support those with disability. Club members could take turns at this, so everybody shares responsibility. At committee level in a club there ought to be an equalities office bearer whose role is to ensure that everybody who wants to be, is included in the life of the club.

These are just a few ideas although with any social or leisure club, it is not good to impose rules of what people must do. However, a balance has to be struck between this and club responsibilities. I hope to rekindle my walking career again. There are many more activities I'd like to achieve. I would like to climb more Munros and would like to experience staying out in a bothy in our beautiful wild places. I hope to find people to do that with who will share that experience with me.

Chapter 10

I think it's fair to say that I've overcome a few barriers in my life both seen and unseen. I would say without a doubt however that the greatest struggle or obstacle that I've come up against has been attitudinal barriers. Whether we name it as prejudice, discrimination or simply ignorance, we all know what it is, and that it is alive and well today. What makes me sad, however, is that it is the same barriers that remain in place today, that prevented me receiving a proper education at school, or entering the employment forum, or taking part in sports all these years ago. In many ways, the emancipation of disabled people has made tremendous progress, particularly in the last decade or so. Although in other ways nothing has changed. For example, if you look at rates of economic activity amongst the disabled population, it really has not improved despite the introduction of equality legislations in the 1990's. Sadly I meet lots of parents of disabled children who go through exactly the same struggles as my parents went through when I was at school all these years ago. I used to campaign and try to change the horizon for disabled people and at one time I thought I would do my bit. I did this through writing, campaigning, sitting on committees and writing to MPs and MSPs. It wasn't making me happy and, to be honest, I don't think it changes anything. Sometimes I think of disabled people as the last minority group. It is as if we are the last group of people in society who will finally receive the same rights of citizenship as everyone else. The way that our society still treats people with learning disabilities is something that was all should be thoroughly ashamed of. They still have among the lowest rates of health outcomes, lowest economic rates, and hate crime against them is actually on the increase. So, despite the undeniable liberation of disabled people, unfortunately it is the tip of the iceberg of what needs to be done.

Today, I feel that the best way for me to make a difference, or make an impact, is just to be out in the world doing what I do and living life on my terms. Society does tremendous damage to people by defining them within the parameters of whatever construct they fit into. Once we realise that these social constructs are not real and we decide to step outside of them, we are truly set free. To live life on our own terms and by our own values is a great joy. It is society that tells disabled people that they are less able or less desirable in some ways. It is in this same way that society has told women that they should behave in such a way. It repulses me that women are still having to fight for equal pay and fair representation at board levels within major organisations. It is the very same attitudes that still keep disabled people out of certain types of jobs, out of politics, and out of public life.

Many people look on their lives and say that they wouldn't change a thing but I'm not one of them. You bet there are loads of things I would change. However, I have no desire at all to look back at my life at the moment at all. I'm so excited about the future and all the things I've done and would like to do. I feel more confident than I ever have. I feel that life has only got better as I've grown older. I do wish I had a fraction of the confidence I have now much earlier than I found it. For example many go off travelling in their 20's and have what they call a 'year out'. I did not do that but feel so up for travelling now and that is exactly one of the things I would like to do in the future. There are so many places I would love to see and it is never too late as they say.

Managing the Future

In order to do the things I would like to do in the future, there are strategies that I know now will help me stay fit, healthy and able. I may never be completely free of mental health issues, many people aren't. What has changed, and I hope will continue to improve, is the way that I manage and cope with my mental health. Now I live with mental health but, given the right tools, can live a more satisfying life. I do regret the mental health difficulties I have experienced; it has held me back tremendously and caused me immeasurable amounts of distress. Today I have to manage them so here are a few of the strategies I use to cope:

Exercise:

Nobody needs me to tell them the benefits of physical exercise on health and well-being. It can't be overestimated. Spending time around nature and just being in the outdoors has helped me a lot. As well as the fresh air, physical exercise makes us feel great no matter how big or small it is. You don't need to run a marathon or climb a mountain to experience the benefits of being outdoors. A wander round a local park area or just round the block can change the course of your day.

I love playing golf, or trying to play golf at least, being out on the golf course is a nice space to be in. I love being in that environment and have met some really lovely people at my home club who are really supportive and welcoming of me. When I'm not golfing, I still love to be by the coast, I need to see the sea on a regular basis/

Mindfulness:

I've found learning and practicing mindfulness to be really helpful. At any given time, all we have is that particular moment and, once we realise that, it can set us free from all sorts of nonsense or unwanted thoughts. The very realisation that our thoughts are just that, and nothing more, puts us halfway there. I have lots of little techniques that I use to bring myself right back to the here and now using my breath. Breathing in and out. Simple yes, but it has really helped me many times. Mindfulness is a process. You are never done with it or it's never complete. It's a discipline that sets us free.

Habits & Rituals:

I had a friend who lived right around the corner from me. He was a champion cyclist and he won many races in his day. I would see him going out to train in all weathers, all through the year. Only the snow or frost would keep him indoors. I used to train as much as I could but nothing compared to him, he would go out cycling regardless. One day we were talking about our training and I said to him, 'how do you keep going in all the nasty weather?' He replied, 'It's just a habit.' He did not realise at the time that this turned out to be one of the best pieces of advice I ever received.

Adopt good habits and keep them. People spend years wishing they could get fit, wishing they could lose weight or stop smoking. Until they take the steps and adopt the habits they need, it will never happen. Take going to the gym as an example. People procrastinate over this. But if your bag is packed and in the car for example, and it is what you do after work, there is no thought involved. It becomes routine, a habit. There are so many things we can put in place to adapt to habits and rituals.

Challenge Belief Systems

I've had to constantly evaluate what I believe about myself.   What we believe about ourselves and what we can do comes from all sorts of places. It can come from childhood or society. Wherever they come from, I have found, they usually turn out to be wrong or based on false evidence. We are led to believe that we can't do things, or a certain career is not for us, or we should live a certain way. However, when we really get down to the root of these beliefs, we find they are built on fresh air. Furthermore, if we go on facts and rely on evidence, we can actually achieve more than we thought possible. The voices that tell us we can't do things are usually silenced by fact.

Vocabulary

I constantly work on my vocabulary, the way I speak about others, but more importantly, the way I speak to myself. The way we talk to ourselves, our internal dialogue is so important and should not be neglected. This is actually one of the things I still struggle with the most. The words we use to describe ourselves and others are so important. When we run down others, we run down ourselves. The importance of choosing your words very carefully cannot be overestimated. Words have a profound and lasting effect.

Change the feed

I love the idea of life being like a Facebook feed or other social media page. You can choose who you follow, choose what you want to see more off and block out the people who drag you down. The people who speak less of you are not worth a place on your page. The more of the positive you feed, the more you see. This little analogy has helped me a lot.

Gratitude

I love the saying "The struggle ends where the gratitude begins". Never a truer word is said. Start and end your day with Gratitude and it changes everything. There seems to be so many people unaware of the privileges and freedoms that we have just by living in the West for example in relative safety and comfort.

There are so many things I would like to do in the future. I would like to see more places and parts of the world. When I was a student, the age where most people go off travelling and exploring the world, I either didn't have the confidence or wasn't well enough to do it. Now I feel fantastic. I really want to travel and see as many places as I can. Until I can though, I feel so blessed to have the life that I do. A few years ago, I'd have bitten your hand off for the opportunity I have now. I still have my down days. I regret that I haven't established a career and the education that my parents fought so hard to get me has not been put to better use. I've tried to do the best with what I have and I know I'll have got it wrong at times but that's what happens. As my Dad used to say "not bad for a slow learner".

Setting out my story in a book like this has been something I have thought about doing for a long time but never gotten around to. Now that I've finally done it, I hope that by doing so, I might help at least one person. It's been a cathartic thing for me to do as well and I hope you have enjoyed reading it as much and I enjoy sharing it with you.

Printed in Great Britain
by Amazon

80378140R00093